THE CATHOLIC UNIVERSITY OF AMERICA
CANON LAW STUDIES
No. 332

THE LAW OF THE CELEBRET

A HISTORICAL SYNOPSIS AND A COMMENTARY

A DISSERTATION

Submitted to the Faculty of the School of Canon Law of the Catholic University of America in Partial Fulfillment of the Requirements for the Degree of Doctor of Canon Law

by

REV. GEORGE F. SCHORR, A.B., J.C.L.
Priest of the Diocese of Columbus

THE CATHOLIC UNIVERSITY OF AMERICA PRESS
WASHINGTON, D. C.
1952

NIHIL OBSTAT:

CLEMENS V. BASTNAGEL, J.U.D.
Censor Deputatus

Washingtonii, D. C., die 26 martii, 1952.

IMPRIMATUR:

✠ MICHAEL J. READY, D.D.
Episcopus Columbensis

Columbi, die 28 martii, 1952.

Printed by
THE ABBEY PRESS
ST. MEINRAD, INDIANA

TO MY FRIENDS

TABLE OF CONTENTS

PART II

CANONICAL COMMENTARY

FOREWORD

"Celebret" is the popular name for the commendatory letters which will obtain for a priest admission to the celebration of Mass in a church other than the one to which he is attached. The Code of Canon Law in canon 804 is very specific in its regulations concerning the qualities, issuance and effect of the celebret, and in its regulations concerning the conditions under which a traveling priest, if he does not have a celebret, may be permitted to offer Mass in a church other than the one to which he is attached. All of these regulations have a common purpose—the safeguarding of the Holy Sacrifice of the Mass.

The Mass is the soul and center of Catholic worship. It is the great treasure of the Church. And throughout its history the Church has watched over the Mass with profound solicitude. Not only has the Church enacted minute directions for the proper and devout celebration of Mass, but it has also done all in its power to prevent irreverence toward the Mass, especially such as would arise from the invalid or illicit offering of Mass.

The legislation of the Church which constitutes the law of the celebret today is contained in canon 804 of the Code of Canon Law. Part Two of this dissertation, that is, the canonical commentary, is limited, then, in scope to a treatment of this canon.

Usually, however, there is an interesting and important history in connection with each of the Church's disciplinary laws. Canon 804, which embodies the law of the celebret, is no exception. The historical description of the Church's legal provisions regarding the celebration of Mass by a traveling priest in a church other than the one to which he was attached forms the scope of Part One of this dissertation, that is, the historical synopsis.

May this dissertation, then, instill in all a greater appreciation of the Mass inasmuch as it reflects the Church's unremitting concern for the proper celebration of the Holy Sacrifice.

This work is placed under the patronage of the Blessed Virgin Mary, Queen of the Clergy.

Sincere thanks is due and is humbly offered to the Most Reverend Michael J. Ready, D.D., Bishop of Columbus, Ohio, for the opportunity to pursue graduate studies in Canon Law at the Catholic University of America; to the members of the Faculty of the School of Canon Law for their devoted assistance; to the members of the Class of 1952 of the School of Canon Law for their inspiring loyalty; and to all who have helped in any way whatsoever in the preparation of this dissertation.

PART I

HISTORICAL SYNOPSIS

INTRODUCTION TO THE HISTORICAL SYNOPSIS

TRAVELING, for one purpose or another, appealed to the early Christians, whether clerics or laymen, just as it has to all peoples throughout history. To aid them in their travels, the early Christians were furnished with introductory letters. St. Paul referred to such documents in writing to the Corinthians.[1]

In the case of laymen, these letters insured their hospitable reception in towns other than their own and made it possible for them to enjoy the rights of all Christians even during their travels.

The use of such letters is attested by early conciliar legislation. The Council of Elvira (305-306) made laws concerning the granting of these letters,[2] and the acceptance of such documents when presented by a traveler.[3]

For clerics, introductory letters had a further purpose. They enabled them to be accepted according to their proper rank and made it possible for the clerics, subject to custom and local regulations, to exercise their respective orders. In the case of a priest this involved, as time progressed, the offering of Mass. The Church of Lyons (ca. 178), according to Eusebius, provided Irenaeus with an introductory letter when he journeyed to Rome.[4]

The protection afforded by such introductory letters to those who received traveling laymen and clerics further justified their existence and use.

Inasmuch as these letters had various purposes and were provided for both clerics and laymen, one should expect to find some variety in the form that they took and in the terms used in reference to them. Then, too, it should be remembered

[1] 2 Cor., III, 1.

[2] Canon 25—Bruns, *Canones Apostolorum et Conciliorum Saeculorum IV-VII* (2 vols., Berolini, 1839), II, 5 (hereafter cited as Bruns).

[3] Canon 58—Bruns, II, 9.

[4] *Historia Ecclesiastica*, Lib. V, cap. 4—Migne, *Patrologiae Cursus Completus, Series Graeca* (161 vols., Parisiis, 1857-1866), XX, 438 (hereafter cited as *MPG*).

that the terminology of the early Church lacked the exactness and precision that would characterize it later on.

A brief consideration of the various references and enactments regarding what was to become the law of the celebret will help to bring each particular point into proper perspective with regard to the whole matter to be treated.

Thus it will be seen that the development and utilization of this institute of introductory letters, in so far as it concerned the offering of Mass by a priest traveling outside his own territory, was intimately connected with the Church's legal history—a small but important thread in the tapestry of the Church's ever glorious canonical life.

CHAPTER I

LEGISLATION PRIOR TO THE COUNCIL OF TRENT

Article 1. Lack of Legislation before 314

From the testimony of St. Ignatius of Antioch († ca. 107)[5] and St. Cyprian († 258),[6] and from the testimony found in the *Canons of Hippolytus of Rome,*[7] and the *Apostolic Constitutions*[8] it is safe to conclude that a priest in the early Church did not offer Mass alone in his own territory very often, since the bishop was the ordinary minister of the Mass.[9] And even fewer were his opportunities, if there were any at all, of celebrating Mass in a church or territory other than his own.

On the other hand, Mass was not offered as frequently in the early Church as is the custom today. Extant testimony on this point indicates that in the beginning Mass was celebrated on Sundays only.[10] Gradually, however, other days

[5] *Ep. ad Smyrnaeos,* cap. 8, n. 2—*MPG,* V, 714; Funk, *Patres Apostolici* (2. ed., 2 vols., Tubingae, 1901), I, 282.

[6] Kurtscheid, *Historia Iuris Canonici, Historia Iinstitutorum,* Vol. I (ab Ecclesiae fundatione usque ad Gratianum) (Romae: Officium Libri Catholici, 1941), p. 57 (hereafter cited as Kurtscheid); Migne, *Patrologiae Cursus Completus, Series Latina* (221 vols., Parisiis, 1844-1855), IV, 232, 263 (hereafter cited as *MPL*).

[7] Canon 20—H.(ans) Achelis, *Die ältesten Quellen des orientallischen Kirchenrechts, I, Die Canones Hippolyti* (Texte und Untersuchungen, VI), (Leipzig, 1891), p. 48.

[8] Funk, *Didascalia et Constitutiones Apostolorum* (2 vols., Paderbornae, 1905), I, 497 (hereafter cited as Funk).

[9] Cf. Kurtscheid, p. 57; cf. *MPG,* V, 714.

[10] Acts, XX, 7; The *Didache* (ca. 90)—*Florilegium Patristicum* (ed. Bernhardus Geyer et Johannes Zellinger, 44 fasciculi, Bonnae: Sumptibus Petri Hanstein, 1911-1941); Fasciculus VII, *Monumenta Eucharistica et Liturgica Vetustissima,* collegit, notis et prolegomenis instruxit Johannes Quasten (Bonnae, 1935), pars I, p. 12 (based on the Funk-Bihlmeyer edition of the *Didache,* 1924) (hereafter cited as *Monumenta*); St. Justin the Martyr (ca. 100-ca. 166)—*Monumenta,* pars. I, p. 19 (an emendation of the Goodspeed-Otto edition of the *Apologia*); *MPG,* VI, 429; Pliny the Younger (62-113), *C. Plinius*

were added for the public celebration of Mass.[11] The Churches at Alexandria and Rome, however, seemed to have continued to have Mass only on Sunday.[12] Evidence of a daily offering of Mass in Africa is found in the testimony of Tertullian († ca. 240)[13] and of St. Augustine († 430).[14]

Nothing certain can be shown about the inception of the custom of private Masses.[15] Even if it did begin very early, it was not sufficiently prevalent to occasion in the early stages of the Church's history the enactment of legislation concerning the offering of Mass by a traveling priest.

This brief consideration, then, of the ordinary minister of the Mass and of the frequency with which Mass was offered in the beginning of the Church helps to explain the lack of canonical regulations during this period regarding the celebration of Mass by traveling priests. As the number of days on which Mass was offered increased, however, and priests began to offer Mass by themselves more frequently, laws were enacted to regulate the acceptance of traveling priests who wished to celebrate Mass.

It should be noted that in this early period the absence of laws demanding that a traveling priest have letters of recommendation did not preclude the existence of such a prac-

Traiano Imperatori, Lib. X, n. 96—The Loeb Classical Library, *Pliny Letters* (2 vols., London: Heinemann, 1935), II, 402.

[11] Epiphanius of Salamis († 403), *Expositio Fidei*, n. 22—*MPG*, XLII, 825; Tertullian († ca. 240), *De Oratione*, c. XIX—*MPL*, I, 1181; *Quinti Septimi Florentis Tertulliani Opera—Corpus Scriptorum Ecclesiasticorum Latinorum* (70 vols., Vindobonae, 1866-), Vol. XX, pars I, p. 192 (hereafter cited as *CSEL*); St. Basil († 379), *Epistola XCIII* (ad Caesariam Patriciam)—*MPG*, XXXII, 484.

[12] Socrates, *Historia Ecclesiastica*, Lib. V, c. 22—*MPG*, LXVII, 638.

[13] *Adversus Marcionem*, Lib. IV, c. 26—*MPL*, II, 425; *Liber de Corona Militis*, c. III—*MPL*, II, 79.

[14] *Sermo XVIII* (De Oratione Dominica)—*MPL*, XXXVIII, 395; *Epistola XCVIII*, n. 9—*MPL*, XXXIII, 364; *S. Aureli Augustini Operum Sectio II, S. Augustini Epistulae—CSEL*, XXXIV, pars II, 530-531.

[15] Gasparri (1852-1934), *Tractatus Canonicus de Sanctissima Eucharistia* (2 vols., Parisiis, 1897), I, n. 66 (hereafter cited as Gasparri).

tice. On the contrary, the appearance of legislation in the fourth century implied that the practice did exist to some extent before specific written legal enactments appeared.

Article 2. Particular Legislation before the Council of Chalcedon (451)

Section I. Conciliar Legislation from 314 to 451

Various particular councils during the period under consideration referred to the exercise of orders by clerics during a temporary stay in a strange city. These councils provided that bishops and priests were to be received as such in a church that they visited and were to be given an opportunity to offer Mass.[16] It was required, however, that the visitors possess an identifying document.[17] Bishops were to secure permission and letters of recommendation from the bishop in the primatial see, and priests, from their bishop, before making a journey.[18] Reference was likewise made to the length of time that a bishop or priest could be absent from his own territory.[19]

[16] I Provincial Council of Arles (314), canon 19—Bruns, II, 109; so-called IV Council of Carthage, i.e., *Statuta Ecclesiae Antiqua*, canon 33—Bruns, I, 145. Concerning this so-called IV Council of Carthage, cf. Van Hove, *Commentarium Lovaniense in Codicem Iuris Canonici*, 1 vol. in 5 toms., Tom. I, *Prolegomena* (2. ed., Mechliniae-Romae: H. Dessain, 1945), pp. 152-153 (hereafter cited as *Prolegomena*). C. 33, C. VII, q. 1.

[17] Council of Antioch in Syria (ca. 332 or 341), canon 7—Mansi, *Sacrorum Conciliorum Nova et Amplissima Collectio* (53 vols. in 60, Parisiis, 1901-1927), II, 1311, 1323 (hereafter cited as Mansi); c. 9, D. LXXI. Concerning the date of this council, cf. *Prolegomena*, p. 143. Council of Laodicea in Phrygia (343/380), canon 41—Mansi, II, 572. Concerning the date of this council, cf. *Prolegomena*, pp. 143-144. I Council of Carthage (348), canon 5—Bruns, I, 113; c. 6, D. LXXI.

[18] III Council of Carthage (397), canon 28—Bruns, I, 127; Council of Laodicea in Phrygia (343/380), canons 41, 42—Mansi, II, 572; c. 36, D. V, *de cons.*

[19] Council of Sardica (343), canons 20, 15—Bruns, pp. 105, 101.

Section II. The APOSTOLIC CONSTITUTIONS

The *Apostolic Constitutions* and the *Canons of the Apostles,* which according to Funk (1840-1907) are the work of one and the same author and were not composed before the year 400,[20] contained important references to the receiving of traveling clerics.

In the second book of the *Apostolic Constitutions,* according to Funk's version, a visitor of at least episcopal rank was to have the opportunity to offer Mass if he so desired.[21] There was no mention made here of commendatory letters being required of visitors, although in the text of the *Apostolic Constitutions* used by Migne (1800-1875) there was,[22] and Funk admits that, even though such letters were not demanded, their necessity was not thereby excluded.[23]

In the eighth book of the *Apostolic Constitutions,* better known as the *Canons of the Apostles,* it was prescribed that no traveling cleric, whether bishop, priest or deacon, was to be received unless he presented commendatory letters, and that the individuals were to be examined as to the purity of their teaching before being accepted. Failure to observe these regulations was to result in a penalty for the one received and the one who received him.[24]

Section III. Letters of Pope Zosimus (417-418)

In a letter addressed to all the Bishops of Gaul Pope Zosimus conferred an unusual privilege on Patroclus, the Bishop of Arles. All ecclesiastics, from any part of Gaul, no matter what their rank, were to obtain the necessary commendatory letters *(litterae formatae)* for traveling from him or his successors. This was to be the case whether they wished to travel to Rome or elsewhere in the world. And without

[20] Funk, I, XVIII-XIX. Concerning the date of composition, cf. *Prolegomena,* p. 129.

[21] Funk, I, 166-168.

[22] *MPG,* I, 738.

[23] Footnote n. 1—Funk, I, 166.

[24] Canons 33, 12—Funk, I, 573, 567.

such letters, granted by the Bishop of Arles, they were not to be received anywhere. These letters were to indicate the bearer's status in the Church, and to prevent impostors from receiving reverence that was in no way due to them. The Pope further stated that if any ecclesiastics from Gaul, of any rank whatsoever, would come to him without the aforementioned letters, they would in no way be received by him. He concluded by attaching to these provisions the penal sanction of an excommunication.[25]

In a later letter addressed to the same bishop, Pope Zosimus reiterated and confirmed his original decree.[26]

Article 3. The Council of Chalcedon (451)

The Council of Chalcedon, the IV Ecumenical Council, marked a focal point in the history of the law of the celebret. In canon thirteen the Council decreed that under no circumstances should traveling clerics and readers *(lectores)* officiate in another city unless they had commendatory letters from their own bishop.[27]

Thus in clear and precise language it determined for the whole Church the condition under which traveling priests could be permitted to offer Mass in a church other than their own. Nothing was indicated about the time element of the travelers' stay in a foreign city. But whether their visit was long or short, they could not offer Mass without the letters which indicated that they were approved by their own bishop.

Canon eleven of this Council confirmed and brought into clear relief the meaning of canon thirteen by distinguishing between the letters of peace, which were to be given to the poor and to those who were in need of help when traveling,

[25] *MPL*, XX, 662; Jaffé, *Regesta Pontificum Romanorum ab condita ecclesia ad annum post Christum natum MCXCVIII* (2. ed., G. Wattenbach, F. Kaltenbrunner, P. Ewald, S. Loewenfeld, 2 vols., Lipsiae, 1885-1888), JK, n. 328 (hereafter cited as JK, JE and JL).

[26] *MPL*, XX, 668; JK, n. 333.

[27] Mansi, VII, 377; c. 7, D. LXXI.

and the commendatory letters, which were to be given to clerics and laymen of high rank.[28]

Article 4. Roman Law

The Emperors Theodosius II (408-450) and Valentinian III (425-455) ordered (ca. 445) that all clerics and monks were to obtain letters from their respective bishops whenever they left their own territory on ecclesiastical business or for some cause connected with religion. If they failed to comply with this regulation, they alone would be responsible for not being accepted elsewhere as clerics and monks.[29] In case the traveler was a priest, then in all likelihood he was not permitted to offer Mass unless he possessed the specified document.

Certain regulations with regard to the travels of bishops were issued by Justinian (527-565). In case it was necessary for bishops to make a journey, they were first to obtain letters from their own patriarch or metropolitan, or obtain an imperial order. No bishop was to absent himself from his church for more than a year. These injunctions were sanctioned with a denial of financial support. In conclusion Justinian indicated that this rule referred to all clerics without regard to their rank or duties.[30]

Article 5. Particular Legislation from 451 to 845

Evidence for the continuity of the law of the celebret is found in various councils during this period. The tenor of this legislation was that a traveling priest must possess commendatory letters.[31]

[28] Mansi, VII, 363. [29] C. (1.3) (22.2). [30] N. (123) 9.

[31] Synod of St. Patrick (450-456), canon 33—Hardouin, *Acta Conciliorum et Epistolae Decretales ac Constitutiones Summorum Pontificum* (12 vols., Parisiis, 1714-1715), I, 1793 (hereafter cited as Hardouin); Mansi, VI, 519; Council of Tours (460), canon 12—Bruns, II, 141; Council of Vannes (465), canon 5—Bruns, II, 143; c. 3, C. XX, q. 4; Council of Agde in South Gaul (506), canon 38—Bruns, II, 153; c. 3, C. XX, q. 4; Council of Epaôn in Burgundy (517), canon 6—Bruns, II, 167; *Monumenta Germaniae Historica*, Legum Sectio III,

An outstanding development during this period was the application of the law requiring commendatory letters of traveling clerics to monks. The Council of Chalcedon (451) had forbidden monks to roam about from city to city and decreed that all monks should be subject to the bishop of the territory in which they lived.[32] Shortly after this, particular legislation required traveling monks to have commendatory letters.[33]

Article 6. The Pseudo-Isidorian Decretals

In the Pseudo-Isidorian Decretals—a clever forgery made on the canvas of the Hispana in the middle of the ninth century—appeared many references to the law of the celebret. Many of these consisted of previous authentic legislation; others, of complete forgeries. All can at least be considered as a reflection of tradition or as evidence of the outlook of the times on the subject being treated.

In the class of authentic legislation belonged the repetition

Concilia, Tomus I, *Concilia Aevi Merovingici* (recensuit Fridericus Maassen, Hannoverae: Impensis Bibliopolii Hahniani, 1893), p. 20 hereafter cited as *MGH*); III Council of Orleans (538), canon 15—Bruns, II, 197; Council of Rheims (625), canon 12—Bruns, II, 263; Mansi, X, 596. Regarding the authenticity of this law, cf. Fournier-Le Bras, *Histoire des Collections Canoniques en Occident depuis les Fausses Décrétales jusqu'au Décret de Gratien* (2 vols., Paris: Recueil Sirey, 1931-1932), I, 262. To the Council of Rouen (650) was attributed a law which belonged to Charlemagne's Capitularies (ca. 769). Council of Rouen, canon 8—Bruns, II, 270; *Caroli Magni Capitularium* I, c. 4—*Monumenta Germaniae Historica* (188 vols., incomplete, Hannoverae, 1826), *Leges in 4*, Sectio II (*Capitularia Regum Francorum*), Tom. I (ed. Alfredus Boretius, 1883), p. 45. Council of Meaux (845), canons 50, 51—Mansi, XIV, 830.

[32] Canon 4—Hardouin, II, 602.

[33] Council of Vannes (465), canon 6—Bruns, II, 143; Council of Agde (506), canon 38—Bruns, II, 153; Council of Angers (453), canon 8—Mansi, VII, 901; Council of Autun (670), canons 7, 19—*MGH*, Legum Sectio III, *Concilia Aevi Merovingici* (recensuit Fridericus Maassen, Hannoverae: Impensis Bibliopolii Hahniani, 1893), pp. 218-219.

in the Pseudo-Isidorian Decretals of such true and pertinent enactments as those of at least eight early councils.[34]

An excerpt from the acts of synods held under Pope Sylvester I (314-335) and a portion of a letter of Pope Anastasius I (399-401) seemed to pertain to the class of complete forgeries. Both were possibly based on a written account of the life of Pope Anastasius.[35]

According to a decree attributed to Pope Sylvester, under no circumstances was an unknown person to be accepted as a cleric unless he was identified as such by the letters of five bishops.[36] Pope Anastasius gave an identical norm to the Bishops of Burgundy and the neighboring bishops.[37]

Article 7. Gratian and the Decretists

The *Decree* of Gratian (ca. 1140) merely evidenced the historicity of the law of the celebret by repeating previous particular and universal law on the subject.[38]

Of particular interest in connection with Distinction XCVIII of the *Decree* is the gloss in regard to canon one which considered among other things: (a) what was the value of the letters received from five bishops when presented by clerics who came from regions so remote that neither the regions themselves nor the seals of the bishops were

[34] I Council of Arles (314), canons 17, 19—Hinschius, *Decretales Pseudo-Isidorianae et Capitula Angilramni* (Lipsiae, 1863), p. 320 (hereafter cited as Hinschius); Council of Antioch (341), canons 7, 8—Hinschius, p. 269; Council of Sardica (343), canons 20, 15—Hinschius, p. 269; Council of Laodicea (343/380), canons 41, 42—Hinschius, p. 273; III Council of Carthage (397), canons 28, 37—Hinschius, p. 299; so-called IV Council of Carthage (398), canon 33—Hinschius, p. 302; Council of Chalcedon (451), canons 13, 11—Hinschius, p. 285; Council of Agde (506), canons 38, 64—Hinschius, pp. 331-332.

[35] Cf. Duchesne, *Le Liber Pontificalis* (2 vols., Paris: Ernest Thorin, 1886-1892), I, 218.

[36] Hinschius, p. 451; JK, between †173-†174, p. 29; c. 1, D. XCVIII.

[37] Hinschius, p. 525; JK, †277; c. 2, D. XCVIII.

[38] I Council of Carthage (348), canon 5—c. 6, D. LXXI; Council of Antioch (341), canon 7—c. 9, D. LXXI; Council of Chalcedon (451), canon 13—c. 7, D. LXXI.

known; (b) what was to be done if the travelers had no letters. The glossator held that: (a) such letters, even if they had a thousand seals, did not possess any value; (b) in the absence of letters, the proof supplied by witnesses would suffice.[39]

Thus, the mentioning in the glosses of the possibility of receiving traveling clerics because of the testimony of witnesses, which possibility was based on the decretal law, presented the only new note with regard to the law of the celebret as referred to in Gratian and the *Glossa Ordinaria.*[40]

Article 8. The Decretals and the Decretalists

Exactitude in reference to and clearness in exposition of the law of the celebret, as well as important and opportune changes, made the period of the decretals and the decretalists an outstanding one in its history.

A decretal of Pope Alexander III (1159-1181), which probably concerned the permanent stay and the public exercise of orders by clerics, whenever their identification and clerical standing were doubtful, stated that the old law concerning the fact of their ordination should be followed,[41] and that the decision regarding them was to be withheld pending a satisfactory investigation of their mode of life and their reception of all preceding orders.[42] But in case these clerics were priests and wished to be received merely as visitors, they were not to be examined so thoroughly and were to be permitted to offer Mass privately, according to the decretalists.[43]

[39] *Glossa Ordinaria,* ad c. 1, D. XCVIII, s. v. *nisi quinque.*

[40] *Glossa Ordinaria,* ad c. 6, D. LXXI, s. v. *sine literis; Glossa Ordinaria,* ad c. 1, D. XCVIII, s. v. *nisi quinque.*

[41] C. 1, 2, 3, 4, D. XCVIII.

[42] C. 1, X, *de clericis peregrinis,* I, 22; JL, n. 13842.

[43] *Glossa Ordinaria,* c. 1, X, *de clericis peregrinis,* I, 22, s. v. *in suspensione;* Hostiensis († 1271) (Henricus de Segusio), *Commentaria in Quinque Decretalium Libros* (5 vols., Venetiis, 1581), lib. I, tit. XXII, c. 1, s. v. *in suspensione* (hereafter cited as Hostiensis); Ioannes Andreae († 1348), *In Quinque Decretalium Libros Novella Commentaria* (5 vols., Venetiis, 1581), lib. I, tit. XXII, c. 1, s. v. *suspensione*

In summing up the dispute which this decretal occasioned relative to the probative value of the seals of bishops on the letters of unknown clerics, Panormitanus properly distinguished between the seals of the bishops who ordained the clerics and those who merely gave their seals as testimonials for the clerics, and between commendatory and dimissorial letters.[44]

A decretal of Pope Innocent III (1198-1216), occasioned by a question of the Patriarch of Jerusalem, indicated that the canonical ordination of totally unknown clerics without commendatory letters had to be proved through letters or witnesses before the Patriarch permitted them to offer Mass publicly, that is, for the people; if such clerics wished to offer Mass out of devotion, they could be permitted to do so privately or secretly.[45] Thus a traveling cleric could establish his status not only by means of commendatory letters, as previous legislation had required, but also through the testimony of capable witnesses. Commentaries on this decretal held that dimissorial letters would be equally acceptable as commendatory letters;[46] the probative value of letters and witnesses was considered equal;[47] and in addition to letters and witnesses, suitable arguments were approved as an acceptable norm in the identifying of traveling clerics.[48]

(hereafter cited as Ioannes Andreae); Panormitanus (1386-1453), *Commentaria in Quinque Libros Decretalium* (5 vols. in 7, Venetiis, 1588), lib. I, tit. XXII, c. 1, n. 1 (hereafter cited as Panormitanus).

[44] Lib. I, tit. XXII, c. 1, n. 1.

[45] C. 3, X, *de clericis peregrinis,* I, 22; Potthast, *Regesta Pontificum Romanorum inde ab anno post Christum natum MCXCVIII ad annum MCCCIV* (2 vols., Berolini, 1874-1875), n. 2994 (hereafter cited as Potthast).

[46] *Glossa Ordinaria* ad c. 3, X, *de clericis peregrinis,* I, 22, s. v. *commendatitiis;* Hostiensis, lib. I, tit. XXII, c. 3, s. v. *sine commendatitiis.*

[47] *Glossa Ordinaria* ad c. 3, X, *de clericis peregrinis,* I, 22, s. v. *per testes;* Hostiensis, lib. I, tit. XXII, c. 3, s. v. *sive per testes;* Ioannes Andreae, lib. I, tit. XXII, c. 3, s. v. *testes;* Panormitanus, lib. I, tit. XXII, c. 3.

[48] *Glossa Ordinaria, loc. cit.;* Hostiensis, *loc. cit.;* Panormitanus, *loc. cit.* Cf. c. 2, X, *de clericis peregrinis,* I, 22; Potthast, n. 2860.

All the conditions just discussed referred to what necessarily preceded the celebration of Mass publicly, that is, for the people.

The outstanding innovation in this decretal, however, was the provision whereby totally unknown clerics without commendatory letters, when they desired to offer Mass out of devotion, could be permitted to do so secretly. This was an evident change from the universal law of the Council of Chalcedon (451) and the particular legislation which had always demanded commendatory letters as the ordinary prerequisite for permitting traveling clerics to offer Mass in a church outside of their own territory.

Article 9. Particular Legislation from 1212 to 1548

An analytical consideration of the legislation of the Council of Paris (1212) and of twelve particular councils relative to the law of the celebret brings to light several points which are worthy of brief mention. The Council of Paris, presided over by a papal legate, has more than the usual particular interest, in that it was a kind of 'rehearsal' for the IV General Council of the Lateran.[49]

In the first place, a rather detailed explanation of the various reasons necessitating regulations relative to the acceptance of unknown traveling clerics was often interwoven with the regulations themselves. The Council held at Marsiac in the Archdiocese of Auch (1326), for example, mentioned that some of the travelers were not canonically ordained, while others had been excommunicated or were apostates, or criminals who out of fear deserted their own bishops and, without regard for God or the good of souls, falsely posed as priests.[50]

[49] Council of Paris (1212), canon 9—Mansi, XXII, 821.

[50] Canon 2—Mansi, XXV, 776. Cf. also Council of Benevento (1331), canon 38—Mansi, XXV, 955; Council of Freising (1440), canon 1—Mansi, XXXII, 3; Council of Toledo (1473), canon 4—Mansi XXXII, 386; Council of Magdeburg (1485)—Mansi, XXXII, 439; Council of Salzburg (1490)—Mansi, XXXII, 498; Council of Cologne (1536), canon 31—Mansi, XXXII, 1221.

In the second place, particular legislation was often more strict than the universal. For in some dioceses the traveling clerics had to obtain the approval of some diocesan official before being permitted to offer Mass in any church in the diocese.[51]

Finally, the councils sanctioned their laws with appropriate penalties. There were spiritual penalties, especially excommunication, for traveling clerics who did not observe the laws for being received, as also for those who received them contrary to the conciliar enactments. Especially new and interesting were the pecuniary fines that were to be invoked against offenders.[52]

Article 10. The Conditions for Obtaining Permission to Offer Mass in an Alien Diocese.

A brief recapitulation of the preceding articles gives one a composite picture of the canonically prescribed conditions for permitting a traveling priest to offer Mass in a church outside his own diocese.

The basic condition, prescribed practically everywhere and at all times, was the possession and presentation of let-

[51] Council of Benevento (1331), canon 38—Mansi, XXV, 955. Cf. also Council of Bourges (1286), canon 6—Mansi, XXIV, 628; Council of Prague (1346)—Mansi, XXVI, 78; Council of Freising (1440), canon 1—Mansi XXXII, 3; Council of Toledo (1473), canon 4—Mansi, XXXII, 386; Council of Magdeburg (1485)—Mansi, XXXII, 439; Council of Salzburg (1490)—Mansi, XXXII, 498; Council of Seville (1512), canon 43—Mansi, XXXII, 617; Council of Augburg (1548), canon 6—Mansi, XXXII, 1301.

[52] Council of Nogara (1303), canon 1—Mansi, XXV, 111; Council of Seville (1512), canon 43—Mansi, XXXII, 617; Council of Salzburg (1490)—Mansi, XXXII, 498. Cf. also Council of Paris (1212), canon 9—Mansi, XXII, 821; Council of Marsiac (1326), canon 2—Mansi, XXV, 776; Council of Benevento (1331), canon 38—Mansi, XXV, 955; Council of Budapest (1279), canon 32—Mansi, XXIV, 285; Council of Prague (1346)—Mansi, XXVI, 78; Council of Freising (1440), canon 1—Mansi, XXXII, 3; Council of Toledo (1473), canon 4—Mansi, XXXII, 386; Council of Magdeburg (1485)—Mansi, XXXII, 439.

ters which identified the bearer as a priest in good standing in his own diocese.[53]

The nomenclature relative to these letters was never strictly uniform. Thus they were called *"litterae," "formatae," "epistolae," "litterae canonicae," "litterae commendatitiae," "litterae dimissoriae,"* and *"litterae testimoniales."* The most frequently used term was *"litterae commendatitiae."*[54]

The fact that various names were used in designation of these letters, coupled with the nature and purpose of such documents, leads one to expect a variety in their form or construction. Furthermore, the legislation demanding such letters did not prescribe the form that they were to take.

One reference to the form for such letters is found in Distinction LXXIII of the *Decree* of Gratian, which Distinction according to the evidence of the oldest manuscripts[55] is a *"Palea,"* that is, it was added to the *Decree* after the time of Gratian. Nothing certain is known about the time of origin of this form, even though it had often been included in earlier collections, such as those of Regino of Prüm († 915), Anselm of Lucca († 1086) and Ivo of Chartres († 1117).[56] It was no longer in use or even considered in the schools of law at the time of the glossators.[57]

In addition to commendatory letters, which often were

[53] Cf., for example, Council of Antioch in Syria (ca. 332 or 341), canon 7—Mansi, II, 1311, 1323; *supra*, p. 5; Council of Chalcedon (451), canon 13—Mansi, VII, 377; *supra*, p. 7; Council of Meaux (845), canons 50, 51—Mansi, XIV, 830; *supra*, p. 8, footnote n. 31; Council of Paris (1212), canon 9—Mansi, XXII, 821; *supra*, p. 13.

[54] The opinion which excludes *"litterae pacificae"* from the aforementioned class of letters is preferred.—Hefele-Leclercq, *Historire des Conciles* (11 vols. in 20, Paris: Letouzey et Ané, 1907-1949), Tomus II, pars II, p. 799; Schroeder, *Disciplinary Decrees of the General Councils: Text, Translation, and Commentary* (St. Louis: Herder, 1937), pp. 102-103.

[55] D. LXXIII, footnote n. 1—Richter-Friedberg, *Corpus Iuris Canonici* (Editio Lipsiensis II, 2 vols., Lipsiae, 1879-1881).

[56] D. LXXIII, footnote n. 3, in the Richter-Friedberg edition of the *Corpus Iuris Canonici.*

[57] *Glossa Ordinaria,* ad D. LXXIII, s. v. *qualiter.*

very carefully examined, the traveling priest himself sometimes had to undergo some species of examination.[58] This was true especially when a priest visited a place far removed from his home diocese. In this situation, the law at the time of Gratian and at the time of the Decretals required the presentation of commendatory letters from five bishops.[59] The decretalists pointed out that the period of probation, as it were, prescribed in connection with the reception of clerics from remote regions, was for those who wished to offer Mass publicly.[60] The trend requiring an examination of some sort was especially noticeable in the particular legislation from 1212 to 1548, when some diocesan official in the place being visited had to indicate his approval of a traveling cleric.[61] It seems safe to conjecture that throughout the whole period a priest from a neighboring diocese was permitted to offer Mass upon simply presenting commendatory letters.

The basic condition of commendatory letters was somewhat relaxed by the legislation of Pope Innocent III, according to which the proof of a priest's status through capable witnesses or suitable arguments became acceptable.[62] One of these three norms was to be used when a traveling priest wished to offer Mass publicly, that is, for the people. But Innocent III made it possible for a traveling priest to offer Mass secretly out of devotion even when none of these norms could be followed.[63]

[58] *Canons of the Apostles*, canon 33—Funk I, p. 573; *supra*, p. 6; Council of Meaux (845), canon 51—Mansi, XIV, 830; *supra*, p. 8, footnote, n. 31.

[59] C. 1, D. XCVIII; c. 1, X, *de clericis peregrinis*, I, 22.

[60] *Glossa Ordinaria*, c. 1, X, *de clericis peregrinis*, I, 22, s. v. *in suspensione*.

[61] *Supra*, pp. 13-14.

[62] C. 2, 3, X, *de clericis peregrinis*, I, 22.

[63] C. 3, X, *de clericis peregrinis*, I, 22.

CHAPTER II

TRIDENTINE AND POST-TRIDENTINE LEGISLATION

Article 1. The Council of Trent (1545-1563)

THE Council of Trent (1545-1563), in the first of its two important references to the law of the celebret, ruled that for the purpose of avoiding irreverence each bishop in his own diocese should forbid that any wandering or unknown priest be allowed to offer Mass.[1]

Evidently this general legislation was intended as the correction of an abuse, namely, that of admitting to the celebration of Mass unknown priests who were often excommunicated, irregular or otherwise unfit, which abuse was sufficiently prevalent in various parts of the Church to merit the attention of an ecumenical council.

This decree was to be enforced by all local ordinaries, acting even as delegates of the Holy See. They could do whatever seemed necessary to them to attain the ends which this decree was designed to achieve, inclusive of the use of censures and other penalties.[2]

The power of the local ordinaries with regard to regulars in this matter was evidenced by the tenor of this part of the decree and by later authentic interpretations of it.[3] The use of penalties was in line with the provisions of previous particular councils.[4]

A consideration of the second reference to the law of the celebret by the Council of Trent brings into sharper focus the meaning of the above-mentioned reference.

[1] Sess. XXII, *de observandis et evitandis in celebratione missae*—Schroeder, *Canons and Decrees of the Council of Trent* (St. Louis: Herder, 1941), p. 423.

[2] Sess. XXII, *de observandis et evitandis in celebratione missae*—Schroeder, *Canons and Decrees of the Council of Trent*, p. 424.

[3] Cf. Chapter II, Article 2—*infra*, p. 19; cf. also Benedictus XIV, *De Synodo Dioecesana* (2 ed., 4 vols., Mechliniae, 1842), Tom. II, lib. IX, cap. XV, n. 5, pp. 392-393.

[4] *Supra*, p. 14.

In a disciplinary canon the council decreed that no bishop should permit any traveling cleric to offer Mass unless the cleric had commendatory letters from his own ordinary.[5] Thus provision was made for the proper reception of a traveling priest in good standing. To insure that he would be allowed to offer Mass in a diocese other than his own, a priest setting out on a journey first had to obtain commendatory letters from his own ordinary. It was incumbent on the bishop of the diocese visited by the traveling priest to make sure that the said traveling priest possessed commendatory letters if he wished to offer Mass in that diocese.

Thus it is seen that an unworthy priest, which seems to have been the meaning attached to the term used in the first reference (*"vagus et ignotus sacerdos"*), was to be excluded from offering Mass, while provision was made for the proper reception of a traveling priest (*"clericus peregrinus"*) who was in good standing in his own diocese. The latter was to be given the opportunity to offer Mass on the fulfillment of the above-mentioned conditions.

There were only minor differences in the enactments of the Councils of Chalcedon (451) and Trent (1545-1563) regarding the law of the celebret. The Council of Trent expressly mentioned the Mass as one of the functions which a traveling priest possessing commendatory letters could perform, and specified the one responsible for permitting or not permitting a traveling priest to offer Mass in an alien diocese, namely, the bishop.[6]

The Council of Trent derogated from the decretal law of Pope Innocent III (1198-1216) with regard to the law of the celebret.[7] No longer could a bishop permit the private celebration of Mass by a traveling priest without commen-

[5] Sess. XXIII, *de ref.*, c. 16—Schroeder, *Canons and Decrees of the Council of Trent*, p. 445.

[6] Council of Chalcedon, canon 13—Mansi, VII, 377; *supra*, p. 6; Council of Trent, sess. XXIII, *de ref.*, c. 16—Schroeder, *Canons and Decrees of the Council of Trent*, p. 445.

[7] C. 3, X, *de clericis peregrinis*, I, 22; *supra*, pp. 12-13.

datory letters. This innovation of Pope Innocent III lasted until the Council of Trent.

Article 2. Instructions of the Sacred Congregations from the Council of Trent (1545-1563) to the Reign of Pope Benedict XIV (1740-1758)

In the period under discussion various Sacred Congregations issued at least six Instructions relative to the law of the celebret. These Instructions exemplified the application of the universal law of the Council of Trent to particular questions and problems. At the same time they constituted rules which lent themselves to universal application.

By way of synthesis it can be pointed out that the Instructions prescribed: 1) the conditions for the reception of traveling diocesan priests in the churches of religious[8] or in the churches under the care of diocesan priests;[9] 2) the conditions for the reception of traveling priests religious in churches under the care of diocesan priests[10] and in churches under the care of priests of the same Order as[11] or of a different Order from[12] that of the travelers; and 3) the use in certain places of a different type of letters, especially dimissorial letters, instead of or in addition to commendatory letters.[13]

[8] S. C. C., *Nullius*, 17 nov. 1594—*Codicis Iuris Canonici Fontes*, cura Emi Petri Card. Gasparri editi (9 vols., Romae: Typis Polyglottis Vaticanis, 1923-1939. Vols. VII-IX, ed. cura et studio Emi Iustiniani Card. Serédi), n. 2277 (hereafter cited as *Fontes*); S. C. S. Off., 11 aug. 1649—*Fontes*, n. 729; S. C. C., 29 nov. 1670—*Fontes*, n. 2819.

[9] S. C. Ep. et Reg., *Comen.*, 27 oct. 1593—*Fontes*, n. 1496.

[10] S. C. Ep. et Reg., *Comen.*, 27 oct. 1593—*Fontes*, n. 1496; S. C. Ep. et Reg., *Feltren.*, 15 febr. 1595—*Fontes*, n. 1532; S. C. de Prop. Fide, 28 iul. 1616—*Fontes*, n. 4433.

[11] S. C. C., *Zacynthen.*, 27 iul, 1626—*Fontes*, n. 2471; cf. S. C. de Prop. Fide, 28 iul. 1626—*Fontes*, n. 4433, footnote; S. C. S. Off., 11 aug. 1649—*Fontes*, n. 729.

[12] S. C. de Prop. Fide, 28 iul. 1626—*Fontes*, n. 4433; S. C. S. Off., 11 aug. 1649—*Fontes*, n. 729.

[13] S. C. Ep. et Reg., *Comen.*, 27 oct. 1593—*Fontes*, n. 1496.

Article 3. The Legislation of Prospero Lambertini as Archbishop of Bologna and as Pope Benedict XIV

Especially distinctive in the history of the law of the celebret was that individual whose legislation had a particular and a universal aspect. Reference is made to the canonist, Prospero Lambertini (1675-1758), who was Archbishop of Bologna (1731-1740) and then head of the Church as Pope Benedict XIV (1740-1758).

In enacting legislation as Archbishop of Bologna, he reflected the common teaching of the Church regarding the law of the celebret. His enactment provided that the document of traveling priests visiting in his territory be very carefully examined, and that constant vigilance be maintained lest an unknown visitor be permitted to offer Mass without first presenting the necessary letters and completely trustworthy testimony concerning his status.[14]

As Pope Benedict XIV, Lambertini's first reference to the law of the celebret concerned local ordinaries enforcing, by any legal means at the time of the canonical visitation or on any other occasion, the Tridentine Decree *"De observandis et evitandis in celebratione Missae,"* which contained a direct reference to the law of the celebret.[15]

In an encyclical letter issued in 1753, Pope Benedict XIV indicated that regulars, on arriving in the missionary territory where they desired to work, were not to offer Mass until they had presented themselves to the Vicar Apostolic in charge and had him approve their documents obtained from their superiors.[16]

Four years later, Pope Benedict XIV, basing his statements on the provisions of the Council of Trent relative to

[14] Benedictus XIV, *Institutiones Ecclesiasticae* (Editio Tertia Latina Veneta, 2 vols., Venetiis, 1788), Tom. I, Institutio XXXIV, § 1, n. IV, pp. 154-155.

[15] Benedictus XIV, const. *Ad militantis,* 30 mart. 1742—*Fontes,* n. 326; *supra,* p. 17.

[16] Benedictus XIV, ep. encycl. *Apostolicum ministerium,* 30 maii 1753—*Fontes,* n. 425.

the law of the celebret and on subsequent authentic applications of these provisions, pointed out that a bishop was not to be concerned about visiting regulars who offered Mass in churches of their own Order located in his diocese. The case was different when traveling diocesan priests wished to offer Mass in such churches. They first had to get the approval of the bishop in whose diocese they were by showing him their commendatory letters.[17]

Finally, Pope Benedict XIV drew attention to the way in which the law of the celebret was strengthened by the aptly devised safeguards, which he mentioned in detail, of St. Charles Borromeo (1538-1584).[18]

Article 4. Particular Legislation from the Council of Trent (1545-1563) to the Code of Canon Law (1918)

Section I. Survey of Particular Legislation

A brief survey of the legislation of provincial councils during this period gives some idea as to what local ordinaries did in carrying out the commission given to them by the Council of Trent, namely, of enforcing its regulations concerning the law of the celebret.[19]

One council merely repeated the universal law requiring a traveling priest, when desirous of offering Mass outside his own diocese, to have commendatory letters.[20] Some councils mentioned that the letters needed to be authentic.[21]

A notable development was that of placing a time limit on commendatory letters. In other words, the traveling priest

[17] Ep. encycl. *Quam grave*, 2 aug. 1757, § 12—Fontes, n. 443.

[18] Ep. encycl. *Quam grave*, 2 aug. 1757, § 13—*Fontes*, n. 443; *infra*, p. 22, footnote n. 23.

[19] Sess. XXII, *de observandis et evitandis in celebratione missae*—Schroeder, *Canons and Decrees of the Council of Trent*, p. 424.

[20] I Provincial Council of Halifax (1857), Decretum XIII, n. 15—*Acta et Decreta Sacrorum Conciliorum Recentiorum, Collectio Lacensis* (7 vols., Friburgi Brisgoviae, 1870-1892), III, 743 (hereafter cited as *Coll. Lac.*).

[21] I Provincial Council of Benevento (1693), tit. VIII, cap. 2—*Coll. Lac.*, I, 31; I Provincial Council of Urbino (1859), pars I, tit. VII, n. 39—*Coll. Lac.*, VI, 18.

had to have letters dated within a certain time.[22] The time limit set by one council varied according to the more or less distantly removed region from which the visitor came.[23]

Besides having commendatory letters from their own ordinaries, traveling priests were required in some places to obtain permission from the local ordinary, or from some official appointed by him, and to have their letters examined.[24]

A very important feature of the particular legislation of this period was the limiting of the number of times a traveling priest with commendatory letters could offer Mass.[25] After the prescribed period of time the ordinaries of the various places had to be consulted.

The power of deans to permit a traveling priest with commendatory letters but without permission from the local ordinary to offer Mass was mentioned in some councils.[26]

[22] I Provincial Council of Benevento (1693), tit. VIII, cap. 2—*Coll. Lac.*, I, 31; Council of Bordeaux (1583), tit. V—Hardouin, X, 1339; Provincial Council of Naples (1699), tit. II, cap. III, n. 7—*Coll. Lac.*, I, 170; Provincial Council of Prague (1860), tit. III, cap. 2—*Coll. Lac.*, V, 463.

[23] I Provincial Council of Milan (1565)—Hardouin, X, 650; I Provincial Council of Milan, pars II—*Acta Ecclesiae Mediolanensis, a Sancto Carolo Cardinali S. Praxedis Archiep. Mediolan. Condita, Frederici Cardinalis Borromaei Archiepiscopi Mediolan. iussu undique diligentius collecta, et edita* (2 vols., 1682-1683. Tom. I, 1682; Tom. II, 1683), I, pars I, p. 9 (hereafter cited as *Acta Ecclesiae Mediolan.*); cf. III Provincial Council of Milan (1573), n. XI—Hardouin, X, 781; *Acta Ecclesiae Mediolan.*, I, pars I, p. 78.

[24] Provincial Council of Auch (1851), cap. VI, n. 126—*Coll. Lac.*, IV, 1195; I Provincial Council of New Granada (1868), tit. II, cap. 6—*Coll. Lac.*, VI, 478; Provincial Council of Narbonne (1609), cap. 20—Hardouin, XI, 21; Provincial Council of Tuam (1817), n. 3—*Coll. Lac.*, III, 762.

[25] Provincial Council of Vienna (1858), tit. II, cap. 6—*Coll. Lac.*, V, 155; Meeting of Bishops at Loreto (1850), sectio I, n. 16—*Coll. Lac.*, VI, 781; Provincial Council of Venice (1859), cap. 23—*Coll. Lac.*, VI, 339.

[26] Provincial Council of Prague (1860), tit. VI, cap. 6—*Coll. Lac.*, V, 557; Provincial Council of Vienna (1858), tit. II, c. 9—*Coll. Lac.*, V, 158.

Likewise, the duty of those in charge of churches to examine the letters of traveling priests was emphasized in various councils.[27]

Punishment for such who did not observe their regulations about permitting traveling priests to offer Mass was prescribed by some councils.[28]

Finally, the Meeting of Bishops at Loreto in 1850 used the term *"celebret"* and indicated that it was widely used in signification of commendatory letters. From this it seems possible to conclude that the term originated or at least began to be commonly used during the period under consideration.[29]

Section II. The Plenary Councils of Baltimore (1852, 1866, 1884)

An Encyclical Letter, issued by the Sacred Congregation for the Propagation of the Faith on April 20, 1873, merits attention in its own right. It is considered in this section because it referred to the legislation of the first two Plenary Councils of Baltimore (1852 and 1866) regarding the law of the celebret.

The Sacred Congregation mentioned the prudent safeguards provided by the first two Plenary Councils of Baltimore for the enforcement of the Tridentine legislation concerning the law of the celebret. Then the Sacred Congregation forcibly commanded all bishops and vicars and prefects apostolic in mission lands, without any subterfuge, to demand of all traveling clerics and priests commendatory letters issued by their own ordinaries.[30]

The complimentary reference made by the Sacred Congregation helps in the interpretation of the legislation on this matter of the first two Plenary Councils of Baltimore.

[27] Council of Bordeaux (1583), tit. V—Hardouin, X, 1339; Provincial Council of Prague (1860), tit. III, cap. 2—*Coll. Lac.*, V, 463.

[28] I Provincial Council of Benevento (1693), tit. VIII, cap. 1—*Coll. Lac.*, I, 31; Provincial Council of Naples (1699), tit. II, cap. II, n. 5—*Coll. Lac.*, I, 170.

[29] Sectio I, n. 16—*Coll. Lac.*, VI, 781; Cf. *infra*, p. 27.

[30] *Fontes*, n. 4884.

In the first of these councils, the pertinent legislation demanded that traveling priests *(vagi et ignoti)* could be received into a diocese with the permission solely of the bishop of the diocese, provided he had previously received letters from the bishop of the traveling priest.[31]

In the II Plenary Council of Baltimore (1866) the bishops of the United States were urged not to permit a priest coming from elsewhere to perform sacred functions unless he had testimonial or dimissorial letters issued by the bishop of the place from which he had come. This permission was not to be granted to any priest if he delayed more than six months in choosing a bishop to whom he would be permanently subject.[32]

It seems, then, from the legislation of these two councils, as well as from the remark of the Sacred Congregation for the Propagation of the Faith, that the temporary as well as the permanent reception of traveling priests was contemplated and regulated by these norms.

One point of concern for the III Plenary Council of Baltimore (1884) was the abuse attendant on the collections being made by numerous priests, diocesan and regular, from other countries. Thus the Council decreed that in the future no one who came to collect money was to be given permission by the rectors of churches to offer Mass even once (which, however, was not to apply to regulars celebrating Mass privately in monasteries of their own Order) until he had received this permission from the ordinary himself.[33]

Article 5. The teaching of the Commentators from the Council of Trent (1545-1563) to the Code of Canon Law (1918)

The commentators were generally agreed on the nature

[31] I Plenary Council of Baltimore, n. 9—*Concilium Plenarium Totius Americae Septentrionalis Foederatae, Baltimori Habitum Anno 1852* (Baltimore: Murphy, 1853).

[32] N. 110—*Concilii Plenarii Baltimorensis II, Acta et Decreta* (Baltimore: Murphy, 1868).

[33] N. 295—*Acta et Decreta Concilii Plenarii Baltimorensis III* (Baltimore: Murphy, 1886).

of commendatory letters, namely, that they were letters given by an ordinary to clerics going on a journey or permanently leaving a diocese. These letters served to make it possible for a traveling priest to offer Mass and perform other sacred functions outside the diocese from which he came. They ordinarily commended the bearer's way of life, character and soundness of doctrine, mentioned the sacred orders he had received and the absence of impediments that could keep him from offering Mass.[34] These letters were to be given for a definite period of time, so that after that period they proved useless.[35]

Traditional reasons for the use of commendatory letters, namely, the forestalling of the great evils arising from the indiscriminate admission of traveling priests to offer Mass in churches outside their own territory and the precluding of the illicit and invalid celebration of Mass, were indicated.[36]

The Council of Trent decreed that a traveling cleric was to obtain commendatory letters from his own ordinary.[37] The commentators explained that regulars were to obtain commendatory letters from their superiors.[38]

Although practically all the commentators stated that the

[34] Pirhing (1606-1679), *Ius Canonicum in Quinque Libros Decretalium* (5 vols. in 4, Dilingae, 1722), Lib. I, tit. 22, n. 1 (hereafter cited as Pirhing); Devoti (1744-1820), *Iuris Canonici Universi Publici et Privati Libri Quinque* (3 vols., Romae, 1803-1815), II, 217 (hereafter cited as Devoti); Leurenius (1646-1723), *Ius Canonicum Universum* (5 vols. in 4, Venetiis, 1729), Lib. I, tit. 22, quaestio DCXLVI (hereafter cited as Leurenius).

[35] Gasparri (1852-1934), I, n. 364.

[36] Van Espen (1646-1728), *Ius Ecclesiasticum Universum* (5 vols., Lovanii, 1753), Lib. I, pars II, sect. I, tit. 5, cap. IX, nn. 1, 2 (hereafter cited as Van Espen); Gonzalez-Tellez († after 1673), *Commentaria Perpetua in Singulos Textus Quinque Librorum Decretalium Gregorii IX* (5 vols., Lugduni, 1673), Lib. I, tit. 22, cap. III, n. 12 (hereafter cited as Gonzalez-Tellez); Pirhing, Lib. I, tit. 22, n. 3.

[37] Sess. XXIII, *de ref.*, c. 16—Schroeder, *Canons and Decrees of the Council of Trent*, p. 445.

[38] Santi (1830-1885), *Praelectiones Iuris Canonici*, cura M. Leitner (1862-1929) (4. ed., 5 vols. in 2, Ratisbonae, 1903-1905), Lib. I, tit. 22, n. 3 (hereafter cited as Santi).

Tridentine law which required traveling priests to have commendatory letters if they wished to offer Mass was to be observed, and that it derogated from the decretal law which permitted an unrecommended priest to offer Mass privately,[39] yet, some held that an unrecommended priest could offer Mass privately.[40] The condition as set by one commentator, namely, that of precluding any monetary gain to be derived from such a permission, was later included in the universal law of the Church.[41]

The commentators commonly excluded the possibility for a traveling priest without commendatory letters to prove his clerical status by offering to take an oath,[42] although they provided for the case of a priest who actually had possessed commendatory letters, but had lost them or was robbed of them, and also for the case of a priest who could not obtain them because of the inaccessibility of his ordinary.[43]

Regulars were bound by the law of the celebret, except when celebrating Mass in churches of their own Order.[44] Local ordinaries could demand to see and examine the com-

39 Reiffenstuel (1642-1703), *Ius Canonicum Universum* (5 vols. in 7, Parisiis, 1864-1870), Lib. 1, tit. 22, nn. 3, 4 (hereafter cited as Reiffenstuel); Giraldi (1692-1775), *Expositio Iuris Pontificii iuxta Recentiorum Ecclesiae Disciplinam* (2 vols., Romae, 1769), Lib. I, pars I, tit. XXII, sect. CXXXVI, cap. I (hereafter cited as Giraldi); Wernz (1842-1914), *Ius Decretalium* (6 vols., Romae, 1898-1914; Vol. III, 1901), III, n. 532 (hereafter cited as Wernz).

40 Pirhing, Lib. I, tit. 22, n. 5; Schmalzgrueber (1663-1735), *Ius Ecclesiasticum Universum* (5 vols. in 12, Romae, 1843-1845), Lib. I, tit. 22, n. 3 (hereafter cited as Schmalzgrueber); Santi, Lib. I, tit. 22, n. 1.

41 "... seclusa qualibet spe lucri, ..."—Santi, Lib. I, tit. 22, n. 1; Can. 804, § 2: "... dummodo nihil ex celebratione ab ecclesia in qua litat, quovis titulo, percipiat. ..."

42 Gonzalez-Tellez, Lib. I, tit. 22, cap. III, n. 12; Pirhing, Lib. I, tit. 22, n. 4; Reiffenstuel, Lib. I, tit. 22, n. 5; Devoti, II, 220; Santi, Lib. I, tit. 22, n. 3; Gasparri, I, n. 369.

43 Reiffenstuel, Lib. I, tit. 22, nn. 5, 6, 7; Leurenius, Lib. I, tit. 22, quaestio DCXLIX; Schmalzgrueber, Lib. I, tit. 22, n. 3; Giraldi, Lib. I, pars I, tit. XXII, sect. CXXXVI, cap. I; Devoti, II, 220, footnote n. 7; Santi, Lib. I, tit. 22, n. 3; Gasparri, I, n. 369.

44 Pirhing, Lib. I, tit. 22, n. 5; Gasparri, I, n. 372.

mendatory letters of traveling priests before they were permitted to offer Mass in churches of regulars, provided the travelers were diocesan priests or priests of a different Order.[45]

Some commentators held that for intrinsic reasons *(per se)* a bishop could not refuse to permit a traveling priest, known or unknown, if he had commendatory letters, to offer Mass in his diocese, since every priest, when duly disposed and free from all impediments, has a right to celebrate Mass by reason of his ordination. For incidental reasons *(per accidens)* a bishop could forbid such a priest to offer Mass, if he knew that scandal would result from the utilized permission.[46]

If a traveling priest without commendatory letters undertook to offer Mass in a church outside his diocese, neither he nor the one who permitted him to do so incurred any stated penalty, at least according to the universal law.[47]

In conclusion it can be mentioned that one commentator, who wrote toward the end of the nineteenth century, indicated that the common name then for commendatory letters was "*celebret.*"[48]

Article 6. The Code of Canon Law (1918) and Subsequent Instructions of the Sacred Congregations

Since the major part of this dissertation concerns the law of the celebret as found in canon 804 of the Code of Canon Law and in the subsequent Instructions of the Sacred Congregations, it will suffice here to make a few remarks about the canon and to mention the subsequent Instructions of the Sacred Congregations.

One would rightly expect to discern a climax in the his-

[45] Pirhing, Lib. I, tit. 22, n. 5; Schmalzgrueber, Lib. I, tit. 22, n. 1; Van Espen, Lib. I, pars II, sect. I, tit. V, cap. IX, n. 9; Wernz, III, n. 532.

[46] Gasparri, I, n. 373; Wernz, III, n. 532, footnote n. 51.

[47] Giraldi, Lib. I, pars I, tit. XXII, sect. CXXXVI, cap. I; Gasparri, I, n. 371.

[48] Gasparri, I, n. 363; cf. *supra*, p. 23.

tory of the law of the celebret in the canon concerning it in the Code of Canon Law promulgated in 1918. But, even a brief consideration of the provisions made by the Code in this matter shows that it is a climax for which one who has followed the history of this important law is prepared. At the same time, the provisions of the Code on this topic are highlighted by such innovations as give a proper tone to the climax.

In its concise but comprehensive reference to the law of the celebret, the Code of Canon Law retains the basic law as found in the Council of Chalcedon (451),[49] in the decretal law of Innocent III (1198-1216),[50] and in the regulation decreed by the Council of Trent (1545-1563).[51]

At least eight references to the law of the celebret are found in Instructions issued by Sacred Congregations subsequent to the Code of Canon Law.

The first of these is contained in a decree of the Sacred Consistorial Congregation. This decree, issued on December 30, 1918, made special regulations concerning priests from Europe and all countries about the Mediterranean Sea who wish to go to America or the Philippine Islands temporarily or permanently.[52]

The Second reference to the law of the celebret is found in a circular letter issued by the Sacred Congregation of the Council on July 1, 1926. This letter was designed to correct certain abuses in connection with the vacations taken by priests outside their own diocese.[53]

The same Sacred Congregation, in a decree issued on July 28, 1931, insisted that pastors were not to permit tra-

[49] *Supra*, p. 7.

[50] *Supra*, pp. 12-13.

[51] *Supra*, pp. 17-19.

[52] Nn. 1, 2, 4, 5—*Acta Apostolicae Sedis, Commentarium Officiale* (Romae, 1909-1929; Civitate Vaticana, 1929-), XI (1919), 40-41 (hereafter cited as *AAS*); Bouscaren, *The Canon Law Digest* (2 vols. and Supplement through 1948, Milwaukee, Wis.: The Bruce Publishing Co., 1934-1943-1949), I, 94-95 (hereafter cited as *Digest*).

[53] N. 6. (a)—*AAS*, XVIII (1926), 313; *Digest*, I, 139.

veling priests without commendatory letters to offer Mass in their churches unless they were attired in clerical dress.[54]

Finally, over a period of eight years, 1929-1937, the Sacred Congregation for the Oriental Church issued five Instructions containing references to the law of the celebret.[55]

[54] *AAS*, XXIII (1931), 337; *Digest*, I, 123.

[55] Decr. *Qua sollerti*, 23 dec. 1929—*AAS*, XXII (1930), 99; *Digest*, I, 17; Decr. *Non raro*, 7 ian. 1930—*AAS*, XXII (1930), 106; *Digest*, I, 24; Decr. *Saepenumero*, 7 ian. 1930—*AAS*, XXII (1930), 108; *Digest*, I, 27; Instr. *Quo facilior*, 26 sept. 1932—*AAS*, XXIV (1932), 344; *Digest*, I, 39; Monitum, 20 iul. 1937—*AAS*, XXIX (1937), 342; *Digest*, II, 3.

PART II

CANONICAL COMMENTARY

CHAPTER III

THE CELEBRET

Article 1. Qualities

Can. 804, § 1. *Sacerdos extraneus ecclesiae in qua celebrare postulat, exhibens authenticas et adhuc validas litteras commendatitias . . . ad Missae celebrationem admittatur. . . .*

THE commendatory letters or the celebret, shown by a priest who asks to celebrate Mass in a church other than the one to which he is attached, must be authentic and still valid. The celebret must be shown to the priest who has charge of the church.

Section I. "[*Sacerdos . . . exhibens*] . . . LITTERAS COMMENDATITIAS . . . [*ad Missae celebrationem admittatur, . . .*]."

The most satisfactory and comprehensive definition of commendatory letters indicates that they are those letters by which the competent superior bears witness to a) the legitimate ordination of a cleric;[1] b) his good moral standing in his own diocese;[2] c) his freedom from any ecclesiastical penalty which excludes the celebration of Mass, as well as his freedom from any irregularity,[3] and d) his consequent commendable status in general.[4]

The ordination referred to, of course, is that to the priesthood, since the primary purpose of commendatory letters is to provide for the celebration of Mass by the bearer of such

[1] Gasparri, I, n. 363; Augustine, *A Commentary on the New Code of Canon Law* (8 vols., Vol. IV, 2. ed., St. Louis: Herder, 1923), IV, 129 (hereafter cited as Augustine); Blat, *Commentarium Textus Codicis Iuris Canonici* (6 vols., Vol. III, pars I, Romae, 1924), III, pars I, 107 (hereafter cited as Blat); Regatillo, *Ius Sacramentarium* (2 vols., Santander: Sal Terrae, 1945-1946), I, 60 (hereafter cited as Regatillo).

[2] Gasparri, I, n. 363.

[3] Gasparri, I, n. 363; Augustine, IV, 129; Blat, III, pars I, 107.

[4] Gasparri, I, n. 363; Blat, III, pars I, 107; Regatillo, I, 60.

letters. The language of the Code of Canon Law does not exclude other purposes for such letters, such as the obtaining of all the faculties of the diocese,[5] yet the scope of this dissertation limits the interest in these letters to their use in obtaining for the bearer permission to offer Mass.

Strictly, then, the various authorities issuing commendatory letters would not have to mention explicitly the bearer's ordination to the priesthood. This could be implied in the course of the letters or could be evident from the purpose of the letters. Ordinarily, however, the fact that the bearer is a priest should be mentioned, since this seems to be more in line with the official nature of commendatory letters.[6]

The competency of a priest to offer Mass is indicated both positively and negatively by commendatory letters.

In a positive way commendatory letters should refer to the good moral standing of the bearer in his own diocese. Although this is not strictly necessary, yet it is highly desirable. At times, though, such reference is inherently precluded, as in the case given by Motry of a priest who had just been absolved from a censure. Motry indicates that it would be appropriate to permit such a priest to celebrate Mass because of the spiritual benefits to be derived thereby, but points out that it would hardly be commensurate with the objective truth to commend him in view of his "good standing."[7] Even if the good standing of such a priest is not mentioned, it would not necessarily militate against him. This is fitting, since one who has fulfilled all the legal requirements for having a censure removed should not have to bear a stigma because of his earlier mistake.

Negatively, commendatory letters should indicate the absence of anything that would prevent a priest from offering Mass legitimately, namely, irregularities or impedi-

[5] Motry, *Diocesan Faculties According to the Code of Canon Law*, The Catholic University of America Canon Law Studies, n. 16 (Washington, D. C.: The Catholic University of America, 1922), p. 54 (hereafter cited as Motry).

[6] Motry, p. 53.

[7] Motry, p. 53.

ments,[8] and ecclesiastical penalties.[9] This element of the commendatory letters is in accord with the purpose of a document which is designed to remove all doubt relative to permitting the bearer to offer Mass.[10]

The actual commendation is not only a welcome feature of any testimonial,[11] but it is important here in so far as it specifies the purpose of commendatory letters, namely, the admission of the bearer to the celebration of Mass.[12] Even though the commendation could be implied from the negative element, namely, the absence of anything that would prevent the legitimate celebration of Mass, yet an explicit commendation is fitting, if not strictly necessary. This commendation may be directed solely to local ordinaries,[13] or, more inclusively, to local ordinaries, rectors of churches and superiors.[14]

A short, appropriate and commonly used name for letters of recommendation is *"celebret."*[15] The exact origin of this term is not determinable. One commentator suggests that it may have come from some ordinary formula or that it may have been taken from the primary purpose of commendatory letters, namely, the admission of the bearer to the celebration of Mass.[16] At any rate the name celebret has been commonly used for commendatory letters at least since towards the end of the nineteenth century.[17] It will be used throughout the rest of this dissertation in designation of commendatory letters, which in the Latin form *"litterae commendatitiae"*

[8] Cf. cans. 968, § 2; 983-991.

[9] Cf. cans. 2261, § 1; 2275, 1°; 2284.

[10] Motry, p. 53.

[11] Motry, p. 53.

[12] Regatillo, I, 60.

[13] Gasparri, I, n. 363.

[14] Regatillo, I, 60; Blat, III, pars I, 107.

[15] Woywood, *A Practical Commentary on the Code of Canon Law* (revised by Callistus Smith, revised and enlarged edition, 2 vols., New York: Jos. F. Wagner, Inc., 1948), I, n. 699 (hereafter cited as Woywod).

[16] Motry, p. 54.

[17] Gasparri, I, n. 363; cf. *supra*, p. 27.

was historically the most commonly used term for the document under consideration.[18]

Relative to the form of the celebret no specific regulations are given by the Code of Canon Law. Therefore, the form is optional.[19] Implicitly, however, the term *"commendatitiae"* seems to require a special formulation for the celebret.[20] According to Motry the ordinary pagella of diocesan faculties would not suffice in and of itself *(per se)* unless it contained a commendatory statement concerning the grantee. In such a case Motry would restrict its use to the diocese of the grantee.[21] With regard to religious, the letters given to them by the proper superior when they travel or change from one house to another would seem to fulfill the requirements for a celebret, provided they embody some pertinent phrase, such as *"valet etiam pro Missa celebranda,"* and fulfill the conditions specified in the Code of Canon Law for every celebret.[22] Any deviation from the ordinary form of the celebret in the case of Oriental priests will be considered in Chapter III, Article 2, Section III. Concerning priests of the Latin rite, inclusive of priests religious who have obtained an indult of exclaustration or of secularization, who wish to go from Europe and all countries about the Mediterranean Sea to America or to the Philippine Islands for an indefinite period of time or permanently, the Sacred Consistorial Congregation has issued special regulations relative to the manner in which the discessorial letters, which would serve the purpose of the celebret, are to be issued. For Italian priests the Sacred Congregation reserves to itself the right to issue the letters. For Spain and Portugal the

[18] Cf. *supra*, p. 15.

[19] Simeone, "Il 'celebret' nel can. 804 e nella prassi," *Miscellanea Francescana*, XLIX (1949), 257.

[20] Motry, p. 54; cf. Cappello, *Tractatus Canonico-Moralis De Sacramentis* (5 vols., Vol. I, 5. ed., Romae: Marietti, 1945), I, 655 (hereafter cited as Cappello).

[21] Motry, p. 54.

[22] Simeone, "Il 'celebret' nel can. 804 e nella prassi," *Miscellanea Francescana*, XLIX (1949), 257; can. 804, § 1.

Papal Legates of these countries have the right to issue the letters.[23]

It can be mentioned here that the oral testimony or commendation of the authority competent to issue the celebret would be an acceptable substitute for the celebret.[24]

By way of summary it can be pointed out that the form of the celebret is optional. Any celebret, however, should indicate at least implicitly that the bearer is a priest, state definitely that he is free from any canonical obstacle to the legitimate celebration of Mass, mention his good moral standing in his own diocese, if such is the case, and commend him to those qualified to examine the celebret. Those things which pertain to the authenticity and validity of the celebret will be considered in Chapter III, Article 1, Section II. A suggested form for a celebret, which embodies all the above mentioned elements will be given in Appendix I.

Section II. "[*Sacerdos* ... *exhibens*] ... AUTHENTICAS ET ADHUC VALIDAS [*litteras commendatitias* ... *ad Missae celebrationem admittatur*, ...]."

To produce the effect ascribed to it by canon 804, § 1, namely, of obtaining for the bearer the permission to offer Mass in a church other than the one to which he is attached, a celebret must be authentic and still valid.

There is basic agreement among the commentators as to what is required for a celebret to be authentic, namely, that it have the signature and the seal of the proper authority.[25]

[23] Nn. 1, 2, 4, 5—*AAS*, XI (1919), 40-41; *Digest*, I, 94-95.

[24] Gasparri, I, n. 369; Coronata, *De Sacramentis Tractatus Canonicus* (3 vols., Vol. I, Taurini-Romae: Marietti, 1943), 147 (hereafter cited as Coronata).

[25] Blat, III, pars I, 107; Ayrinhac, *Legislation on the Sacraments in the New Code of Canon Law* (New York: Longmans, Green & Co., 1928), p. 85 (hereafter cited as Ayrinhac); Duskie, *The Canonical Status of the Orientals in the United States*, The Catholic University of America Canon Law Studies, n. 48 (Washington, D. C.: The Catholic University of America, 1928), p. 102 (hereafter cited as Duskie); Crnica, *Commentarium Theoretico-Practicum Codicis Iuris Canonici* (2 vols., Vol. II, pars I, Šibenik: Typis Typographiae "Kačić", 1941),

According to some commentators, however, either the seal, or the signature, or some other indication of genuineness or authenticity would suffice.[26] As an example of what may constitute such an indication Motry mentions an accompanying picture of the episcopal coat of arms, the wording of the letterhead, and the official form of the document. But he adds that such an indication must be confirmed by collateral proof.[27] A third group combines elements of the preceding two opinions. Thus Vermeersch-Creusen mention the seal and other indications,[28] while Cappello says that a celebret should be issued by the ecclesiastical superior as such and according to the proper form.[29]

Since a secular priest is to obtain his celebret from his own ordinary, and a priest religious, from his superior, and a priest of an Oriental rite, from the Sacred Congregation for the Oriental Church,[30] the signature on a celebret should be respectively that of the ordinary, of the religious superior, or of a delegate of either, or of one of the officials of the Sacred Congregation for the Oriental Church.[31] The seal should be respectively that of the ordinary, that is, either his personal seal or that of the diocese, that used by the religious superior, or that of the Sacred Congregation for the Oriental Church.[32]

In view of the above mentioned opinions, then, a celebret

II, pars I, 37 (hereafter cited as Crnica); Jombart, "Celebret," *Dictionnaire de Droit Canonique* (Paris: Letouzey et Ané, 1924-), III, 129 (hereafter cited as *Dictionnaire de Droit Canonique*); Coronata, I, 147; Henry, *The Mass and Holy Communion: Interritual Law,* The Catholic University of America Canon Law Studies, n. 235 (Washington, D. C.: The Catholic University of America Press, 1946), p. 74 (hereafter cited as Henry).

[26] Motry, p. 52; Regatillo, I, 61.

[27] Motry, p. 52.

[28] *Epitome Iuris Canonici* (3 vols., Vol. II, 6. ed., Mechliniae-Romae: H. Dessain, 1940), II, 41 (hereafter cited as Vermeersch-Creusen).

[29] Cappello, I, 655.

[30] Can. 804, § 1.

[31] *Dictionnaire de Droit Canonique*, III, 129; Coronata, I, 147.

[32] Coronata, I, 147.

which is so drawn up that it is recognized as such and which has the signature and the seal of the proper authority is to be considered authentic. Augustine (1872-1943) rightly remarked that celebrets are to be presumed genuine until the contrary is proved.[33] This is in accord with the canonical norms concerning the cogency of credit value attaching to public ecclesiastical documents.[34]

Concomitantly with the authenticity of a celebret must be considered its validity. A celebret can become invalid through any one of four causes, namely, through the completion of the period of time for which it was issued, through the non-verification of a condition upon which its validity depends, through revocation, or through the bearer's rendering himself unworthy to offer Mass.

The Code of Canon Law requires that a celebret to be effective be still valid, but it does not indicate the length of time for which a celebret remains valid,[35] nor does it limit the time for which a celebret may be issued.[36]

It is evident, and many authors point this out that, if a celebret is issued for a definite period of time and if that period has elapsed, then the celebret is no longer valid.[37]

Duskie holds that a celebret is by its nature temporary,[38] and Gasparri (1852-1934) noted that a celebret is usually given for a determined period of time.[39] Augustine men-

[33] Augustine, IV, 131.

[34] Cf. cans. 1813 and 1814.

[35] Can. 804, § 1; Augustine, IV, 131.

[36] Can. 804, § 1.

[37] Gasparri, I, n. 368; Blat, III, pars I, 107; Duskie, p. 102; Crnica, II, pars I, 37; *Dictionnaire de Droit Canonique*, III, 129; Coronata, I, 147; Romani, *Institutiones Iuris Canonici* (2 vols., Vol. II, pars I, Romae, 1944), II, pars I, n. 195 (hereafter cited as Romani); Cappello, I, 655; Regatillo, I, 61; Henry, p. 74; Claeys Bouuaert-Simenon, *Manuale Juris Canonici* (3 vols., Vol. II, 3. ed., Gandae et Leodii: Dessain, 1947), II, n. 79 (hereafter cited as Claeys Bouuaert-Simenon); Simeone, "Il 'celebret' nel can. 804 e nella prassi," *Miscellanea Francescana*, XLIX (1949), 258.

[38] Duskie, p. 102.

[39] Gasparri, I, n. 368; cf. Woywod, I, n. 701.

tioned that a celebret is usually issued for one year, but that the authority issuing it may lengthen or shorten this period.[40] Yet the Code of Canon Law does not explicitly require that a celebret be issued for a specifically predetermined period of time.[41] Therefore, it is left to the prudent judgment of the authority issuing it to determine the period of time for which the celebret is valid,[42] if he sets any time limit at all.[43]

In practice, however, a celebret is ordinarily issued for a definite period of time. The purpose for which a priest is going to be away from his church will usually be the determining factor. Such things as vacationing, seeking the recovery of one's health, pursuing study, undergoing correction, undertaking business, making a pilgrimage, or other considerations of a similar or different nature may be the reason for a priest temporarily or for a considerable length of time to leave the church to which he is attached.[44] From this can be seen the wisdom of the Code of Canon Law in not determining the period of time for which a celebret may be issued. Parenthetically it can be stated that it is not necessary to indicate on a celebret the reason why the bearer is away from the church to which he is attached, although this is sometimes done,[45] and indeed seems a laudatory practice.

Some commentators, according to Regatillo,[46] hold that a celebret is invalid after six months. They base their argument on the parity between the celebret and the testimonial letters required by canon 964 for ordination. Regatillo admits that a celebret *can* be valid for any length of time, but thinks that an ordinary or the rector of a church would not act imprudently in refusing to honor a celebret that is more

[40] Augustine, IV, 131.

[41] Can. 804, § 1.

[42] Duskie, p. 102.

[43] Coronata, I, 147; Cappello, I, 655; Regatillo, I, 61.

[44] Motry, p. 52.

[45] Celebret of the Diocese of Columbus, Ohio: "... testamur———— sacerdotem Dioeceseos Columbensis, qui ex causa———— ... a Nostra Dioecesi aberit, ...".

[46] Regatillo, I, 61.

than six months old.[47] Such an action, however, seems to be contrary to the norm of canon 804, § 1, which does not place any limit on the time for which a celebret may be issued. Simeone suggests that a celebret be renewed at least once a year or even every six months, but is careful to point out that it is necessary to consider a celebret given at any date valid, even though given several years before, provided, of course, that it was not given for any definite period of time.[48] It is imperative to keep in mind also the provision of the Code of Canon Law for the celebration of Mass by a priest without a celebret.[49]

If a celebret is issued with some condition attached and that condition is not fulfilled, the celebret is invalid.[50]

Motry aptly remarks that a time-limit dependent upon the fulfillment or non-fulfillment of a certain condition should not be construed as in any way derogatory to the character of the bearer of such a celebret, nor as incompatible with the concept of a commendatory document.[51] The same principle would also apply to a simple time-limit placed on a celebret.

A third way for a celebret to become invalid is through revocation.[52] The authority issuing a celebret, or also the superior, the successor of that authority, or one delegated by any of these to issue and to revoke a celebret, would be competent to revoke it.[53] The nature of the case and the urgency of the revocation would determine the steps to be taken to make this revocation effective. It would simplify the matter if the proper authority wishing to revoke a celebret

[47] Regatillo, I, 61.

[48] "Il 'celebret' nel can. 804 e nella prassi," *Miscellanea Francescana*, XLIX (1949), 258.

[49] Can. 804, § 2.

[50] Such a condition might be the wearing of the clerical garb.—Motry, p. 52; Coronata, I, 147; Cappello, I, 655; Regatillo, I, 61.

[51] Motry, p. 52.

[52] Blat, III, pars I, 107; Romani, II, pars I, n. 195.

[53] Omnis res, per quascunque causas nascitur, per easdem dissolvitur.—c. 1, X, *de regulis iuris*, V, 41.

knows the whereabouts of the bearer of a celebret which is to be revoked. The speed and efficiency of modern methods of communication and the world-wide organization of the Church should facilitate this matter.

A celebret automatically becomes invalid and the time-limit, if any, on it is not to be taken into consideration if the bearer renders himself unworthy to celebrate Mass.[54] The causes for the revocation and the automatic invalidation of a celebret are practically co-extensive. The nature of these causes and any differences between them, as well as other points pertaining to the revocation and the automatic invalidation of a celebret, will be discussed in Chapter III, Article 3, Section II.

Section III. "SACERDOS EXTRANEUS ECCLESIAE IN QUA CELEBRARE POSTULAT . . . [*ad Missae celebrationem admittatur, . . .*]."

Every priest must belong either to some diocese or to some religious institute.[55] This being the case, it can normally be expected that every priest will be attached to a particular church or oratory of a diocese or of a religious institute, in which ordinarily he will celebrate Mass.

What, then, is the meaning of the opening phrase of canon 804, § 1, that is, "*sacerdos extraneus ecclesiae in qua celebrare postulat, . . . ?*" Commentators agree that the term "*sacerdos extraneus*" does not refer merely to extra-diocesan priests. Of itself it also applies to any priest who is not legitimately connected in any way with the church in which he desires to celebrate Mass.[56] The matter was succinctly

[54] Motry, pp. 49-50; Augustine, IV, 131; Duskie, p. 102; Romani, II, pars I, n. 195; Henry, p. 74.

[55] Can. 111, § 1; Romani, II, pars I, n. 195.

[56] Augustine, IV, 129; Motry, p. 48; Blat, III, pars I, 107; Pejška, *Ius Canonicum Religiosorum* (3. ed., Friburgi Brisgoviae: Herder, 1927), p. 264 (hereafter cited as Pejška); Duskie, p. 102; Wernz-Vidal, *Ius Canonicum ad Codicis Norman Exactum* (7 vols. in 8, Vol. IV, *De Rebus*, pars I, Romae: Apud Aedes Universitatis Gregorianae, 1934), IV, pars I, n. 72 (hereafter cited as Wernz-Vidal); *Dictionnaire*

put by Woywod (1880-1941), who, in his translation of canon 804, § 1, referred to a priest who desires to say Holy Mass in a church *other than that to which he is attached.*[57]

Thus the term *"sacerdos extraneus"* would include not only every priest who is a stranger in the diocese, but also every priest who is a stranger at the church where he desires to celebrate Mass. It would exclude, of course, the pastors and vicars of churches, priests in residence at a church, and chaplains of hospitals and religious communities.[58]

It should be remembered, also, that the mere fact that a priest is not incardinated in the diocese wherein he actually resides does not make him a *"sacerdos extraneus."* Urgent missionary needs, specialized work or other important reasons could necessitate his residence in a diocese other than his own. Such a priest would be subject to the jurisdiction of the local ordinary because of his newly acquired domicile or quasi-domicile.[59] Nevertheless, such a priest could be a stranger with regard to some church in the diocese wherein he is residing. In this section of the dissertation also it is necessary to keep in mind the provisions of canon 804, § 2, concerning the celebration of Mass by a priest who has no celebret.

At least one commentator clearly points out that canon 804, § 1, refers solely to the celebret of priests. He bases his argument on the terms of the law itself and stresses the point that no mention whatsoever is made of any requirements for

de Droit Canonique, III, 128-129; Romani, II, pars I, n. 195; Regatillo, I, 60; Henry, p. 74; Cance, *Le Code de Droit Canonique* (7. ed., 3 vols., Paris: J. Gabalda, 1946), II, 256 (hereafter cited as Cance); Simeone, "Il 'celebret' nel can. 804 e nella prassi," *Miscellanea Francescana*, XLIX (1949), 264; Eichmann-Mörsdorf, *Lehrbuch des Kirchenrechts auf Grund des Codex Iuris Canonici* (3 vols., Vol. II, *Sachenrecht*, Paderborn: Schöningh, 1950), II, 43 (hereafter cited as Eichmann-Mörsdorf). Cappello holds that canon 804 refers directly and immediately only to extra-diocesan priests.—I, 656.

[57] Woywod, I, n. 699.

[58] Cf. *Dictionnaire de Droit Canonique*, III, 128-129.

[59] Duskie, p. 102; cf. cans. 91, 92, 94.

the admission of a bishop to the celebration of Mass. Further, he indicates that the case in which a traveling bishop who as someone unknown to the rector of the church and without authentic indications of his office requests admission for the celebrating of Mass is exceptionally rare, and is in fact well provided for in canon 804, § 2, if any timidly conscientious interpreter of the law would classify bishops among those meant by the Code of Canon Law as "*sacerdotes extranei.*"[60]

Besides being mentioned in a reference to the Sacred Congregation for the Oriental Church, the word "*ecclesia*" or church occurs four times in canon 804. Blat correctly indicates that a church of the Latin rite is meant,[61] but he does not seem to go as far as Jombart, who says that canonical equity demands that the word *church* throughout canon 804 should be understood in a broad sense so as to include every oratory wherein Mass can be celebrated, for otherwise the law would be of little efficacy.[62] It is true that canon 804 expressly mentions only churches. This would certainly include public oratories,[63] and, in the law under consideration, very likely it would include semi-public oratories,[64] and even private oratories.[65]

Section IV. "[*Sacerdos*] . . . EXHIBENS . . . [*litteras commendatitias . . . ad Missae celebrationem admittatur, . . .*]."

Canon 804, § 1, directly concerns the efficacy of the celebret, and indirectly, its necessity. If a celebret is to produce

[60] Motry, pp. 53-54.

[61] Blat, III, pars I, 107; cf. can. 1.

[62] *Dictionnaire de Droit Canonique*, III, 129; Blat, III, pars I, 107; cf. Feldhaus, *Oratories*, The Catholic University of America Canon Law Studies, n. 42 (Washington, D. C.: The Catholic University of America, 1927), p. 68 (hereafter cited as Feldhaus); cf. Mothon, II, 73.

[63] Can. 1191, § 1.

[64] Drumm, *Hospital Chaplains*, The Catholic University of America Canon Law Studies, n. 178 (Washington, D. C.: The Catholic University of America Press, 1943), p. 51 (hereafter cited as Drumm).

[65] *Dictionnaire de Droit Canonique*, III, 129.

its primary effect, that is, the obtaining for the bearer his admission to the celebration of Mass, then it is evident that it must be shown to someone. This is at least implied by the word "*exhibens*" in canon 804, § 1, and by the very nature of a celebret. To whom, then, is the celebret to be presented?

According to canon 804, §§ 1 and 2, it is not necessary to first present the celebret to the ordinary of the place where the bearer wishes to offer Mass. In other words, the common law makes no such demand.[66] The question as to whether or not a local ordinary could prescribe this will be discussed in Chapter V, Article 1, Section. II.

In the first paragraph of canon 804 there is no indication as to the one who is to examine a celebret, but in the second paragraph of this canon reference is made to the rector of the church as admitting to the celebration of Mass the priest who has no celebret. It is manifest, then, that the rector of the church is to examine the celebret.[67] At least two commentators indicate that the rector of the church has an obligation to examine the celebret.[68] Coronata holds that the rector of the church, who would admit a priest to the celebration of Mass contrary to the provisions of canon 804, would be guilty of a sin, which sin would be a serious one "*in materia gravi.*"[69]

It has already been stated that the term *church* in canon 804 is to be interpreted in a broad sense so as to include all types of oratories.[70] The term *rector* should evidently also

66 *Dictionnaire de Droit Canonique,* III, 129.

67 Woywod, "Answers to Questions," *The Homiletic and Pastoral Review,* XXXIV (1933-1934), 73-74; *Dictionnaire de Droit Canonique,* III, 129; Romani, II, pars I, n. 195; Regatillo, I, 61; Simeone, "Il 'celebret' nel can. 804 e nella prassi," *Miscellanea Francescana,* XLIX (1949), 260; Eichmann-Mörsdorf, II, 43. Cf. Gasparri, I, n. 370.

68 Clancy, *The Local Religious Superior,* The Catholic University of America Canon Law Studies, n. 175 (Washington, D. C.: The Catholic University of America Press, 1943), p. 133 (hereafter cited as Clancy); Simeone, "Il 'celebret' nel can. 804 e nella prassi," *Miscellanea Francescana,* XLIX (1949), 260; cf. Romani, II, pars I, n. 195.

69 Coronata, I, 148.

70 *Supra,* p. 44.

be understood in a wide sense in consideration of the purpose of the law enacted in canon 804, §§ 1 and 2.[71] There is need for the common law to control the celebration of Mass by priests in an oratory to which they are not attached, even though it is not as great perhaps as the need for a similar control with regard to a church.[72] Even though one argued that a priest has no right to offer Mass in a semi-public or private oratory to which he is not attached, yet this does not preclude the possibility of his asking to do so. In the case of a hospital chapel, for example, which is ordinarily a semi-public oratory, there will usually be many such requests because of the peculiarily public character of a hospital.

Besides its technical meaning as found in canon 479, then, the term *rector* includes pastors, quasi-pastors in mission countries, and parochial vicars who have full parochial power,[73] with regard to parochial churches and the oratories or chapels dependent on them,[74] and chaplains or rectors with regard to oratories.[75] One can probably sum up the matter best by stating that the celebret should be shown to the priest in charge of the church or the oratory.[76] Other priests could be delegated by those in charge of churches or oratories to examine any celebret presented.[77]

Relative to the celebret of a priest who desires to offer Mass in the churches or oratories of women religious or of lay communities of men, a question arises as to the one who is to examine the celebret, that is, the chaplain or the religious superior or superioress. From what has been said in the preceding paragraph and from the consideration that it is unbecoming for a priest to be subject in this regard to

[71] Can. 18.

[72] Drumm, p. 51.

[73] Can. 451, §§ 1 and 2.

[74] *Dictionnaire de Droit Canonique*, III, 129.

[75] Cf. cans. 479, § 2, and 529; *Dictionnaire de Droit Canonique*, III, 129; Eichmann-Mörsdorf, II, 43.

[76] Woywod, I, n. 699; cf. Blat, III, pars I, 108.

[77] *Dictionnaire de Droit Canonique*, III, 129.

one who is not a priest, it can be concluded that the logical one to examine the celebret is the chaplain.[78]

It sometimes happens, though, that the superior of a lay community of men or the superioress of a community of women religious will permit a traveling or visiting priest to offer Mass without having the chaplain or the pastor, if the church or oratory is dependent on him, examine the priest's celebret. Likewise, in some cases, a lay sacristan is permitted to examine the celebret.[79] Both of these practices are not only unbecoming, but also contrary to the common law as found in canon 804 and to its proper interpretation.[80] The circumstances which would permit even the toleration of such an occurrence would be rare indeed, and it would certainly be necessary that the superior, superioress or sacristan have adequate information concerning the law of the celebret.[81]

With regard to private oratories, it is necessary to distinguish between those of the laity and those of priests. In those of priests, the right of offering Mass is limited to the priest for whose convenience in celebrating Mass the indult was granted, while in those of the laity, any priest having the ordinary faculty to offer Mass in a diocese and any priest with a celebret can be requested to offer the single Mass (*Missa unica*) that is allowed.[82] In the latter case the celebret should be examined by the chaplain of the oratory, if there is one, or by the priest in charge of the church in whose territory the oratory is located, or by the priest who ordinarily celebrates Mass in the private oratory.

Article 2. Source

> Can. 804, § 1. *Sacerdos . . . exhibens . . . litteras commendatitias sui Ordinarii, si sit saecularis, vel sui Superioris, si religiosus, vel Sacrae Congrega-*

[78] Woywod, "Answers to Questions," *The Homiletic and Pastoral Review*, XXXIV (1933-1934), 73-74.

[79] *Dictionnaire de Droit Canonique*, III, 129.

[80] Eichmann-Mörsdorf, II, 43.

[81] *Dictionnaire de Droit Canonique*, III, 129.

[82] Feldhaus, p. 129.

tionis pro Ecclesia Orientali, si ritus orientalis, ad Missae celebrationem admittatur, ...

The celebret is to be obtained from the proper authority. For a secular priest the proper authority is his ordinary; for a priest religious, his superior; and for a priest of an Oriental rite, the Sacred Congregation for the Oriental Church.

Section I. "[*Sacerdos . . . exhibens . . . litteras commendatitias*] SUI ORDINARII, SI SIT SAECULARIS, . . . [*ad Missae celebrationem admittatur, . . .*]."

Canon 804, § 1, explicitly states that a secular priest is to obtain his celebret from his ordinary. In referring to this matter, most commentators merely repeat the words of the canon.[83] Since canon 804, § 1, prescribes that the priest religious is to obtain the celebret from his religious superior, it is clear that here the term *ordinary* is to be understood in the sense of *local ordinary*,[84] and includes, for secular priests, all local ordinaries mentioned in can 198.[85]

According to canon 111, § 1, every priest must belong either to some diocese or to some religious institute or community. By means of incardination a secular priest becomes linked with his diocese and thus obtains his ordinary.[86] It is from such an ordinary, then, that a secular priest could normally be expected to secure his celebret.

This is the primary meaning of the requirement of canon 804, § 1, that a secular priest obtain his celebret from his ordinary. But, is this interpretation to be considered as an exclusive one? There seems to be sufficient reason to hold that it is not.

[83] Augustine, IV, 129; Motry, p. 54; Blat, III, pars I, 107; Ayrinhac, p. 84; Vermeersch-Creusen, II, 41; Crnica, II, pars I, 37; Romani, II, pars I, n. 195; Henry, p. 74; Cance, II, 256.

[84] Crnica, II, pars I, 37; Regatillo, I, 61; Simeone, "Il 'celebret' nel can. 804 e nella prassi," *Miscellanea Francescana*, XLIX (1949), 257.

[85] Cappello, I, 655. A dean (*vicarius foraneus*) may issue the celebret only if such power is given to him by the ordinary.—Augustine, IV, 130, footnote n. 16.

[86] Cans. 111, § 2-117.

Canon 94, § 1, states that a person acquires his proper pastor and ordinary through domicile or quasi-domicile. It is evident that incardination and domicile or quasi-domicile are two distinct institutes which sometimes have reciprocal relations. So it is possible, then, for a priest to have a domicile or a quasi-domicile in a diocese other than the one in which he is incardinated and thus to acquire another proper ordinary.[87] Various reasons, such as teaching or doing special work, could be the occasion for this. Could, then, this second proper ordinary issue a celebret for the priest thus subjected to his jurisdiction? An affirmative answer seems to be in order. For, besides having jurisdiction over the priest in the proposed case,[88] the second ordinary would have, or could easily, and likely, in the case of a protracted stay in his territory, with greater facility than the ordinary of the diocese in which the priest is incardinated, secure the information necessary to issue the celebret. Thus it seems possible to so interpret the term "*sui ordinarii*" in canon 804, § 1, that it would include an ordinary besides the ordinary of the diocese in which a secular priest is incardinated.[89]

An interesting question, concerning which no mention is made in canon 804, is whether or not the competent authority could refuse to issue the celebret. A careful search reveals no treatment of this question among post-Code commentators. Among the pre-Code authors, however, it was generally held that an ordinary could not refuse to issue the celebret, when, for some legitimate reason, he was requested

[87] Cans. 91, 92 and 94.

[88] Can. 94.

[89] A confirmatory argument can at least be inferred from the explanation by Simeone that the ordinary referred to in canon 804, § 1, is the ordinary of the territory from which the bearer of the celebret departs.—"Il 'celebret' nel can. 804 e nella prassi," *Miscellanea Francescana*, XLIX (1949), 257.

Cf. *infra*, p. 60, where it is argued that a priest of an Oriental rite, who, while remaining incardinated in his own Oriental diocese, is subject by reason of domicile to a Latin ordinary or an ordinary of his own rite outside his own Patriarchate or his own Oriental country, must obtain his celebret from such an ordinary.

to do so. Nevertheless, whenever the departure of the priest could be impeded according to the norms of canon law, an ordinary could refuse to issue the celebret.[90] Evidently the request for a celebret by a priest who could not legitimately offer Mass could be refused.[91] Finally, the pre-Code authors held that if the conduct of a priest were reprehensible, but not such as to exclude him from exercising his orders, then, if he were otherwise free to leave, he should be given a celebret which merely shows that he is a priest and is free from irregularities or impediments or ecclesiastical penalties which would keep him from offering Mass.[92]

The principles proposed in the preceding paragraph would apply to any authority competent to issue the celebret, as long as due allowance were made, of course, for the special provisions in the constitutions of religious institutes.

Section II. "[*Sacerdos . . . exhibens . . . litteras commendatitias*] . . . SUI SUPERIORIS, SI [*sit*] RELIGIOSUS, . . . [*ad Missae celebrationem admittatur, . . .*]."

The common law prescribes that a priest religious is to obtain his celebret from his superior.[93] Two questions must be answered concerning this provision of the Code of Canon Law: Who are included in the term "*priest religious,*" and, which religious superior is competent to issue the celebret?

A *priest religious* is one who has made profession of vows in any religious institute,[94] and is still attached to the insti-

[90] Leurenius (1646-1723), Lib. I, tit. 22, quaestio DCXLIX; Schmalzgrueber (1663-1735), Lib. I, tit. 22, n. 2; Giraldi (1692-1775), Lib. I, pars I, tit. XXII, sect. CXXXVI, cap. I; Santi (1830-1885), Lib. I, tit. 22, n. 5; Gasparri (1852-1934), I, n. 368; cf. S. C. C., *Segnen. decretor.*, 22 nov. 1749—*Thesaurus Resolutionum Sacrae Congregationis Concilii* (167 vols., Urbini, 1718-1741; Romae, 1741-1908), XIV, 70.

[91] Pirhing (1606-1679), Lib. I, tit. 22, n. 3; Gasparri, I, n. 368.

[92] Pirhing, Lib. I, tit. 22, n. 3; Leurenius, Lib. I, tit. 22, quaestio DCXLIX; Schmalzgrueber, Lib. I, tit. 22, n. 2.

[93] Can. 804, § 1.

[94] Can. 488, 7°; Augustine, IV, 130; *Dictionnaire de Droit Canonique*, III, 129.

tute.[95] The vows could be either simple or solemn;[96] the institute could be exempt or non-exempt,[97] approved by the Holy See or simply by an episcopal ordinary,[98] and the institute could be either clerical or lay.[99]

A priest who belongs to a society whose members imitate the manner of life of religious by living in a community under the government of superiors according to approved constitutions, but are not bound by the usual three public vows, is not a priest religious in the proper sense.[100] Strictly, then, according to canon 804, § 1, it would be necessary for such a priest to obtain his celebret from his local ordinary. The competent local ordinary would be the one who, as his proper bishop, ordained him or issued dimissorials for his ordination,[101] or the one who is the ordinary of the place in which is located the house to which the priest is attached.[102]

Nevertheless, it can be argued that the superior of the priest is competent to issue the celebret. The nature of the celebret as well as the purpose of the law of the celebret favors his competency, since the superior knows his subjects and is capable of testifying to the fact that the person in question is a priest and can offer Mass legitimately. Likewise, the principle of autonomy in affairs of internal government indicates the competency of the superior.[103]

[95] Cf. cans. 637-645; Blat, III, pars, I, 108.

[96] Can. 488, 2°.

[97] Can. 488, 2°; Pejška, p. 264.

[98] Can. 488, 3°.

[99] Can. 488, 4°; Pejška, p. 264.

[100] Can. 673; Creusen-Ellis-Garesché, *Religious Men and Women in the Code* (4. ed., Milwaukee: Bruce, 1940), n. 18.

[101] Augustine, IV, 131; Stanton († 1941), *De Societatibus sive Virorum sive Mulierum in Communi Viventium sine Votis* (2. ed., Halifaxiae: apud Custodiam Librariam Maioris Seminarii a Sanctissimo Corde B. V. M., 1936), p. 117 (hereafter cited as Stanton); Ristuccia, *Quasi-Religious Societies*, The Catholic University of America Canon Law Studies, n. 261 (Washington, D.C.: The Catholic University of America Press, 1949), p. 163 (hereafter cited as Ristuccia).

[102] Rothoff, *Le Droit des Sociétés sans Voeux* (Brugis: Desclée De Brouwer, 1949), p. 180 (hereafter cited as Rothoff).

[103] Rothoff, p. 180.

A cogent argument can be drawn from the fact that most of the societies have obtained from the Holy See the privilege of allowing their superiors to issue dimissorials for the ordination of their own subjects. By virtue of this privilege a society becomes subject to the legislation governing the ordinations of religious. In view of this fact and because the dependence of the members of the society on their superiors is in other ways the same as that of religious, there seems to be sufficient reason for believing that the superior is competent to issue the celebret.[104]

A corroboratory argument is based on the fact that the prescriptions of the decree *Inter reliquas,* issued by the Sacred Congregation for Religious on January 1, 1911,[105] concerning military service, applied also to societies which have neither solemn nor simple vows, but only simple promises binding their members to the society.[106] In a private reply of the Sacred Congregation for the Propagation of the Faith, this same decree was declared applicable to a society without vows subject to this Congregation.[107]

The arguments here adduced lead to the conclusion, then, that a priest who is a member of a society without vows as described in canon 673 may obtain his celebret from his superior.

There are sufficient reasons to conclude, also, that a priest who is a novice in any religious institute would be included in the term *priest religious* with regard to the law of the celebret. It is true that a novice is not a religious in the strict sense of the term,[108] but a novice shares in all the spiritual privileges of religious,[109] and is expressly likened to a relig-

[104] Stanton, p. 117; Ristuccia, p. 163.

[105] *AAS,* III (1911), 37; *Digest,* I, 106.

[106] N. 9—*AAS,* III (1911), 39; *Digest,* I, 108.

[107] *Sylloge praecipuorum documentorum recentium Summorum Pontificum et S. Congregationis de Propaganda Fide necnon aliarum SS. Congregationum Romanarum ad usum missionariorum* (Romae: Typis Polyglottis Vaticanis, 1939), n. 170; *Digest,* II, 52.

[108] Can. 488, 7°.

[109] Can. 567, § 1.

ious by the Code of Canon Law in several instances.[110] Moreover, a novice is generally better known to his religious superior than to the local ordinary, and thus the former would be well qualified to issue the celebret.[111]

In requiring that a priest religious obtain his celebret from his superior, the Code of Canon Law does not explicitly state which superior is meant.[112] Hence arises the controversy as to whether the term *"sui superioris"* includes the local superior as well as the major superior. Some commentators merely repeat the words of the canon.[113] At least one commentators mentions only the major superior.[114] Most commentators, however, when they treat the question at all, indicate that the local superior is competent to issue the celebret.[115] It is worth noting that Cappello, who formerly reserved this right to the major superior, now admits also the competency of the local superior.[116]

An argument favoring the competency of the local superior can be found in pre-Code references to the law of the celebret. The Council of Trent (1545-1563) decreed that no bishop should admit any traveling priest to the celebration of Mass unless he had commendatory letters from his own ordinary.[117] Since this decree was of a general nature, it applied to regulars,[118] and *a fortiori* to all religious. Spe-

[110] Cans. 514, 875, 1221, 1245, § 3; *Dictionnaire de Droit Canonique*, III, 129.

[111] *Dictionnaire de Droit Canonique*, III, 129.

[112] Can. 804, § 1.

[113] Augustine, IV, 130; Henry, p. 74.

[114] Cance, II, 256.

[115] Blat, III, pars I, 107; Pejška, p. 264; *Dictionnaire de Droit Canonique*, III, 129; Clancy, p. 131; Romani, II, pars I, n. 195; Cappello, I, 655; Regatillo, I, 61; Simeone, "Il 'celebret' nel can. 804 e nella prassi," *Miscellanea Francescana*, XLIX (1949), 264.

[116] *Tractatus Canonico-Moralis de Sacramentis* (3 vols. in 6, Vol. I, 2. ed., Taurinorum Augustae: Marietti, 1928), I, n. 737, 1; cf. Cappello, I, 655.

[117] Sess. XXIII, *de ref.*, c. 16; Schroeder, *Canons and Decrees of the Council of Trent*, p. 455.

[118] Gasparri, I, n. 372.

cific references also were made to religious in the obtaining of the celebret from their superiors.[119] The Council of Trent required the testimony of each priest's ordinary.[120] The power given to local superiors over their subjects by Pope St. Pius V (1566-1572), however, was of such a nature that it can be safely concluded that the local superior could issue the celebret required by the Council of Trent.[121] References to the testimony *"superiorum suorum,"* without any distinction, by Pope Benedict XIV,[122] by the Sacred Congregation of the Holy Office,[123] and by the Sacred Congregation of Bishops and Regulars[124] confirm this conclusion. Among the pre-Code authors no treatment has been found relative to which superior was competent to issue the celebret.[125]

Usually the post-Code commentators in treating this question merely mention that the term *"sui superioris"* of canon 804, § 1, includes the local superior. Two of the commentators,[126] however, propose convincing arguments which are worthy of at least a brief presentation.

According to Clancy, who considers specifically the local superior in religious orders of men, one can see from an

[119] Benedictus XIV (1740-1758), ep. encycl. *Apostolicum ministerium,* 30 maii 1753, § 6—*Fontes,* n. 425; S. C. S. Off., 11 aug. 1649—*Fontes,* n. 729.

[120] Sess. XXIII, *de ref.,* c. 16; Schroeder, *Canons and Decrees of the Council of Trent,* p. 445.

[121] Const. *Romani Pontificis,* 21 iul. 1571, § 3—*Bullarum Diplomatum et Privilegiorum Romanorum Pontificum Tauriensis Editio* (24 vols. et Appendix, Augustae Taurinorum, 1857-1872), VII, 931 (hereafter cited as *BRT*).

[122] Ep. encycl, *Apostolicum ministerium,* 30 maii 1753, § 6—*Fontes,* n. 425; Ep. encycl. *Quam grave,* 2 aug. 1757, § 12—*Fontes,* n. 443.

[123] 11 aug. 1649—*Fontes,* n. 729.

[124] *Comen.,* 27 oct. 1593—*Fontes,* n. 1496; *Feltren.,* 15 febr. 1595—*Fontes,* n. 1532.

[125] Clancy, p. 131; cf. Bouix (1808-1870), *Tractatus de Jure Regularium* (3. ed., 2 vols., Parisiis, 1883), II, 188; Piatus Montensis (1815-1904), *Praelectiones Juris Regularis* (3. ed., 2 vols., Tornaci, 1906), II, 239; Wernz (1842-1914), III, n. 532.

[126] Jombart, *Dictionnaire de Droit Canonique,* III, 129; Clancy, pp. 131-132.

examination of the text of canon 804, § 1, that the legislator has made an evident distinction between the secular priest and the priest religious; the former needs the celebret of his own *ordinary,* the latter, that of his own *superior.* If the legislator wished only the religious ordinary to be the competent superior, it would appear that he would have employed the words *"sui Ordinarii"* instead of *"sui Superioris"* as did the Council of Trent when treating this matter,[127] or that he would have used the words *"Ordinarii proprii"* as referring to the ordinary of either the secular priest or the priest religious.[128]

The next argument is based on the fact that the legislator did not distinguish between superiors. Such a distinction is often made in the Code and could easily have been made here by means simply of the qualifying word *"maioris."*[129]

Moreover, neither the nature of the celebret nor the purpose of the law of the celebret demands the intervention of a major superior.[130] The final argument refers to the right which the conventual prior seems to have enjoyed by privilege under the pre-Code legislation by reason of the quasi-episcopal power given to him in the constitution of St. Pius V, *Romani Pontificis.*[131] It appears that the legislator incorporated this right in canon 804, § 1.[132]

In view of these arguments, then, the competency of the local superior to issue the celebret seems well established. It should be noted, however, that the constitutions of a religious institute or of a society whose members are not bound by vows may determine the circumstances under which,

[127] Sess. XXIII, *de ref.,* c. 16; Schroeder, *Canons and Decrees of the Council of Trent,* p. 445.

[128] Clancy, pp. 131-132.

[129] *Dictionnaire de Droit Canonique,* III, 129; Clancy, p. 132.
In both of these citations reference is made to Cappello, who formerly held that a local superior was without competence to issue the celebret. Cf. *supra,* p. 53.

[130] *Dictionnaire de Droit Canonique,* III, 129; Clancy, p. 132.

[131] 21 iul. 1571—*BRT,* VII, 931, § 3.

[132] Clancy, p. 132.

as well as the time for which, the local superior may issue the celebret.[133] Likewise, the constitutions, if they are approved by the Holy See,[134] may restrict, in favor of the provincial superior or some other major superior, the right to issue the celebret.[135]

Section III. "[*Sacerdos . . . exhibens . . . litteras commendatitias*] . . . SACRAE CONGREGATIONIS PRO ECCLESIA ORIENTALI, SI SIT RITUS ORIENTALIS, . . . [*ad Missae celebrationem admittatur, . . .*]."

A priest of an Oriental rite must obtain his celebret from the Sacred Congregation for the Oriental Church.[136] Even though the Code of Canon Law makes no distinction, as it does in the case of priests of the Latin rite, it is clear that both secular priests and priests religious of the Oriental rites are bound by this law.[137]

In general it can be stated that a priest of an Oriental rite needs a celebret from the Sacred Congregation for the Oriental Church whenever he wishes to offer Mass in a church of the Latin rite, in a church of any Oriental rite other than his own, or in a church of his own rite to which he is not attached, at least outside his own patriarchate or his own Oriental country.[138]

The competency of the local ordinary, whether of the Latin

133 Stanton gives an example of a society whose constitutions allow a local superior to give a member of the society permission to be absent from the Community for a month. In this case Stanton thinks that the superior could issue the celebret for that period of time.—Stanton, p. 117.

134 Cf. can. 489.

135 Can. 488, 8°.

136 Can. 804, § 1.

137 S. C. Or., decr. *Qua sollerti*, 23 dec. 1929—*AAS*, XXII (1930), 99; *Digest*, I, 17; S. C. Or., decr. *Non raro*, 7 ian. 1930—*AAS*, XXII (1930), 106; *Digest*, I, 24; S. C. Or., instr. *Quo facilior*, 26 sept. 1932—*AAS*, XXIV (1932), 344; *Digest*, I, 40; Blat, III, pars I, 108; Romani, II, pars I, n. 195.

138 S. C. Or., instr. *Quo facilior*, 26 sept. 1932—*AAS*, XXIV (1932), 344; *Digest*, I, 40; Augustine, IV, 129-130; Duskie, p. 103.

rite or of an Oriental rite, to issue the celebret to an Oriental priest staying outside his own patriarchate will be considered later on in this section.

Before treating particular questions concerning the celebret of priests of Oriental rites, one may fittingly make a brief mention of the reasons for the apparent stringency of the law in their regard. Primarily, it is to prevent cases of fraud, which have not been infrequent.[139]

Before the Code it frequently happened that men claiming to be priests of an Oriental rite appeared in American countries and in other regions. They had a celebret which apparently was signed and sealed by their ordinaries. Because the celebrets were written in an Oriental language unintelligible to Latin ordinaries and rectors of churches, it was impossible for them to determine whether or not the bearers were Catholic priests who could legitimately celebrate Mass, whether they were schismatics, whether they were lay persons disguised as priests, or whether the documents were forged. Since all these possibilities were verified at one time or another, and since it often happened that these individuals engaged in practices which were scandalous to the faithful, and were at times even permitted to offer Mass in virtue of their unintelligible and, in many cases, false celebrets, the Holy See found it necessary to require Oriental priests to obtain their celebrets from the Sacred Congregation for the Oriental Church.[140] It is this law that is now embodied in the Code of Canon Law.[141]

On July 20, 1937, the Sacred Congregation for the Oriental Church referred in an admonition to reports it had received that certain men, fraudulently exhibiting false credentials and using the name and dress of Oriental priests, were wandering about through various lands, begging alms, collecting

[139] Regatillo, I, 61.

[140] S. Cong. de Prop. Fide, 12 apr. 1894—*Collectanea S. Congregationis de Propaganda Fide* (2 vols., Romae: Typographia Polyglotta S. C. de Propaganda Fide, 1907), n. 1866 (hereafter cited as *Coll.*); Duskie, p. 103.

[141] Can. 804, § 1; Duskie, p. 103.

Mass stipends, and even demanding the right to celebrate Mass.[142]

To impedé the deplorable consequences of these grievous and most sacrilegious impostures, the Sacred Congregation for the Oriental Church urgently begged local ordinaries to call to mind and observe the regulations and decrees which the Holy See had often promulgated with a view to preventing impositions and wrongs of this kind.[143]

These decrees prescribe among other things that no Oriental priest may be admitted to celebrate Mass outside his own patriarchate unless he presents an authentic and still valid celebret issued by the Sacred Congregation for the Oriental Church.[144]

An analysis of these decrees indicates that provisions have been made for several possible situations, each of which will be considered briefly with regard to the law of the celebret.

The first case to be considered is that of Oriental priests, whether secular or religious, who go from their own Oriental countries or dioceses to countries of North, Central or South America or to Australia to administer to the spiritual needs of the faithful of their own rite.[145]

Such an Oriental priest must be approved by the Sacred Congregation for the Oriental Church, and must receive from this Sacred Congregation a celebret which will be valid

[142] S. C. Or., monitum, 20 iul. 1937—*AAS*, XXIX (1937), 342; *Digest*, II, 3.

[143] S. C. Or., monitum, 20 iul. 1937—*AAS*, XXIX (1937), 342; *Digest*, II, 3. The decrees referred to were the following: S. C. Or., decr. *Qua sollerti*, 23 dec. 1929—*AAS*, XXII (1930), 99; *Digest*, I, 17; S. C. Or., decr. *Non raro*, 7 ian. 1930—*AAS*, XXII (1930), 106; *Digest*, I, 24; S. C. Or., decr. *Saepenumero*, 7 ian. 1930—*AAS*, XXII (1930), 108; *Digest*, I, 27; S. C. Or., instr. *Quo facilior*, 26 sept. 1932 —*AAS*, XXIV (1932), 344; *Digest*, I, 39.

[144] S. C. Or., monitum, 20 iul. 1937—*AAS*, XXIX (1937), 342; *Digest*, II, 3; cf. can. 804, § 1.

[145] S. C. Or., decr. *Qua sollerti*, 23 dec. 1929—*AAS*, XXII (1930), 99; *Digest*, I, 17.

for the time required for the journey.[146] For the purpose of avoiding all doubt or difficulty on the part of the bishop of the diocese to which the Oriental priest is going to establish his domicile, the Sacred Congregation for the Oriental Church will send notice concerning the priest to the bishop through the legate of the Roman Pontiff in the country, or, if the matter is urgent, directly to the bishop, but send notice at the same time to the legate of the Roman Pontiff.[147]

The Oriental priest is to proceed without delay to the designated diocese. If, however, it is necessary to interrupt the journey for a time, the priest may be permitted to offer Mass upon presenting his celebret to the rector of the church where he wishes to celebrate Mass. The rector must note on the celebret the date of the celebration of the Mass, the name of the church, and sign it. If the Oriental priest stays longer than seems proper, the rector should notify the local ordinary. The local ordinary should no longer admit to the celebration of Mass an Oriental priest who stays longer than is proper at any intermediate point on his journey, or who without reason goes about from place to place. The local ordinary, moreover, is to report the matter to the Apostolic Nuncio or Delegate, or to the Sacred Congregation for the Oriental Church.[148]

When the Oriental priest arrives at his designated diocese he must present himself to the local ordinary and show his celebret from the Sacred Congregation for the Oriental Church and his discessorial letters from his own bishop or patriarch. The local ordinary is authorized according to the provisions of the rescript he has received from the Sacred Congregation for the Oriental Church, to give the priest permission to celebrate Mass or the divine Liturgy, and to perform all other priestly offices necessary or useful for the

[146] S. C. Or., decr. *Qua sollerti,* 23 dec. 1929, n. 8—*AAS,* XXII (1930), 103; *Digest,* I, 21.

[147] S. C. Or., decr. *Qua sollerti,* 23 dec., 1929, n. 7—*AAS,* XXII (1930), 103; *Digest,* I, 21.

[148] S. C. Or., decr. *Qua sollerti,* 23 dec. 1929, n. 9—*AAS,* XXII (1930), 103; *Digest,* I, 21-22.

spiritual care of the Oriental faithful. The Oriental priest is subject to the jurisdiction of the ordinary of that place where he establishes his domicile, while remaining incardinated in his original Oriental diocese. He must obey all the orders of the local ordinary, whether he be an ordinary of the priest's rite or of the Latin rite. If the Oriental priest wishes to go to another diocese to visit the faithful of his rite living there or to exercise his ministry temporarily, he must first obtain the permission of the ordinary of the diocese where he has his domicile and also the permission of the ordinary whose diocese he wishes to enter.[149]

Since the celebret issued by the Sacred Congregation for the Oriental Church is valid only for the time required for the making of the journey to his new diocese, who is to be regarded as competent for issuing the celebret to the Oriental priest in question when he wishes to offer Mass outside his own church? The Oriental priest is subject to the jurisdiction of the local ordinary, whether of the Latin or of an Oriental rite, and receives from him the permission to offer Mass and to perform all the other priestly offices. Likewise, the local ordinary where the Oriental priest has his domicile is best qualified to issue the celebret, since he should know whether his subjects are worthy of it. For these reasons it is correct to assume that the local ordinary, whether of the Latin or of an Oriental rite, is the proper authority to issue the celebret to the Oriental priest when he wishes to offer Mass outside the church to which he is attached.[150]

[149] S. C. Or., decr. *Qua sollerti,* 23 dec. 1929, nn. 10-12—*AAS,* XXII (1930), 103-104; *Digest,* I, 22.

[150] S. C. Or., decr. *Qua sollerti,* 23 dec. 1929, nn. 8, 10—*AAS,* XXII (1930), 103-104; *Digest,* I, 21-22; Duskie, pp. 104-105; Diederichs, *The Jurisdiction of the Latin Ordinaries Over Their Oriental Subjects,* The Catholic University of America Canon Law Studies, n. 229 (Washington, D. C.: The Catholic University of America Press, 1946), pp. 91-92 (hereafter cited as Diederichs); Henry, pp. 75-76.

Evidently the provision mentioned above would hold with regard to an Oriental priest who is incardinated in a diocese outside his own native Oriental diocese or patriarchate.—Cf. Diederichs, p. 91.

The next case concerns Oriental priests, whether secular or religious, who go from Oriental countries or dioceses to countries of North, Central or South America or to Australia, not for the purpose of caring spiritually for the faithful of their own rite, but for some other cause, economic or moral, or simply to stay there for a short time. Such a priest must obtain a celebret from the Sacred Congregation for the Oriental Church and, as regards intermediate points on the journey to and from the designated place, observe, in so far as they are applicable, the provisions outlined in the previous case.[151] The ordinary of the place to which the Oriental priest goes to stay according to the permission of the Sacred Congregation for the Oriental Church can permit him to offer Mass according to the rescript which the ordinary has previously received from the Sacred Congregation for the Oriental Church. If the local ordinary has not received the rescript, or if the Oriental priest extends his stay beyond the time stated in the rescript, the ordinary may not permit the Oriental priest to offer Mass and should refer the case to the Apostolic Nuncio or Delegate of his country, or to the Sacred Congregation for the Oriental Church.[152]

Regulations similar to the ones discussed in the two previous cases govern the advent and stay of any priest of an Oriental rite, whether he be a regular or a secular, in foreign countries other than those mentioned above and outside his own patriarchate or his own Oriental country.[153]

The final case to be considered is that of Oriental priests collecting or begging alms, money or Mass stipends outside of Oriental countries and dioceses. To engage in any of these activities, an Oriental priest must have permission from the Sacred Congregation for the Oriental Church, whose policy

[151] S. C. Or., decr. *Non raro*, 7 ian. 1930, nn. 3, 5—*AAS*, XXII (1930), 107; *Digest*, I, 25-26; S. C. Or. decr. *Qua sollerti*, 23 dec. 1929, n. 9—*AAS*, XXII (1930), 103; *Digest*, I, 21-22.

[152] S. C. Or., decr. *Non raro*, 7 ian. 1930, nn. 3, 5, 6—*AAS*, XXII (1930), 107; *Digest*, I, 25-26.

[153] S. C. Or., instr. *Quo facilior*, 26 sept. 1932—*AAS*, XXIV (1932), 344; *Digest*, I, 40.

it is never to grant such permission. If, however, because of extraordinary circumstances, such permission is granted, the Holy See will inform the local ordinary either directly or through the legate of the Roman Pontiff, and this without prejudice to the rule that even in this case the collection cannot be made except with the consent of the local ordinary.[154] The local ordinary likewise has the right to examine the document of an Oriental priest in such a case and to decide upon its validity.[155] To obtain permission to offer Mass, the Oriental priest must present a celebret issued by the Sacred Congregation for the Oriental Church.[156]

With regard to the United States of America, the III Plenary Council of Baltimore (1884) decreed that priests from abroad who came to collect alms without proper authorization were not allowed to celebrate Mass even once without the permission of the local ordinary.[157] Canon 804 separates the qualifications for the celebration of Mass from those requisite for the taking up of collections.[158] Moreover, this decree of the III Plenary Council of Baltimore seems to be a restriction of the right of the rector of a church to permit an unknown priest to celebrate Mass once or twice,[159] and thus, being opposed to the Code of Canon Law, is, according to canon 6, 1°, abrogated.[160]

According to canon 622, § 4, local ordinaries of the Latin rite may not permit any Oriental religious to collect money

[154] S. C. Or., decr. *Saepenumero*, 7 ian. 1930, nn. 1-4—*AAS*, XXII (1930), 109; *Digest*, I, 27-28.

[155] Can. 51.

[156] S. C. Or., monitum, 20 iul. 1937—*AAS*, XXIX (1937), 342; *Digest*, II, 3; can. 804, § 1.

[157] N. 295—*Acta et Decreta Concilii Plenarii Baltimorensis* III (Baltimore: Murphy, 1886).

[158] Hannan, "Cases and Studies," *The Jurist*, VIII (1948), 453.

[159] Can. 804, § 2.

[160] Barrett, *A Comparative Study of the Councils of Baltimore and the Code of Canon Law*, The Catholic University of America Canon Law Studies, n. 83 (Washington, D. C.: The Catholic University of America, 1932), p. 127; Hannan, "Cases and Studies," *The Jurist*, VIII (1948), 452-454. Duskie holds the opposite opinion on this matter.—Duskie, pp. 106-107.

in their territory without an authentic and recent rescript from the Sacred Congregation for the Oriental Church. Previous to the Code of Canon Law, a decree, which makes no distinction between Oriental priests secular or religious who come to America to collect alms, required that such priests have the approval and permission of the Holy See. Otherwise, the local ordinary is strictly forbidden to allow them to perform sacred functions.[161] The local ordinary has the right to examine the Oriental priest's document and to decide upon its validity.[162]

By way of summary of this somewhat detailed section, it can be stated: (1) that a priest of an Oriental rite, when he goes to a country outside his own patriarchate or Oriental country to administer to the spiritual needs of the faithful of his own rite, must have a celebret from the Sacred Congregation for the Oriental Church for presentation on his arrival to the local ordinary, whether of the Latin or of an Oriental rite, to whom he is to be subject; (2) that a priest of an Oriental rite, when he, outside his own patriarchate or Oriental country is subject to the jurisdiction of a local Latin or an Oriental ordinary of his own rite, must obtain his celebret from the respective ordinary in whose diocese he has established his domicile for the purpose of administering to the spiritual needs of the faithful of his own rite; (3) that a priest of an Oriental rite, when he is merely visiting a country outside his own patriarchate or Oriental country, or has gone there for any purpose other than that of administering to the faithful of his own rite and thus is not the subject of any ordinary in that country, must bring with him his celebret and credentials obtained from the Sacred Congregation for the Oriental Church.

Article 3. Effect.

Can. 804, § 1. *Sacerdos ... exhibens authenticas et adhuc validas litteras commendatitias ... ad Missae celebrationem admittatur, nisi interim aliquid*

[161] S. Cong. de Prop. Fide, 12 apr. 1894—*Coll.*, n. 1866.
[162] Can. 51.

eum commisisse constet, cur a Missae celebratione repelli debeat.

The effect of an authentic and still valid celebret is the obtaining for the priest bearing it of admission to the celebration of Mass, unless it is known that since the celebret was issued the bearer has done something for reason of which he must be kept from celebrating Mass.

Section I. "[*Sacerdos . . . exhibens authenticas et adhuc validas litteras commendatitias*] . . . AD MISSAE CELEBRATIONEM ADMITTATUR, . . ."

Canon 804, § 1, implicitly contains the general rule that a priest who wishes to offer Mass in a church other than the one to which he is attached should have a celebret. Explicitly, however, it concerns the efficacy of the celebret.[163]

Some commentators observe that the law of the celebret has as one of its purposes the fostering of a spirit of fraternal charity among priests.[164] The particular concern here, however, is whether or not the celebret confers on the bearer the right to offer Mass in a church other than the one to which he is attached.

By reason of ordination a priest, if he is rightly disposed and not bound by any irregularity, impediment or ecclesiastical penalty which would prevent him from legitimately offering Mass, has the right to celebrate Mass. The Church may either command or urge the recognition of this right.[165]

Pre-Code legislation relative to the celebret was negative in form.[166] It did not consider the positive case in which a priest possesses a celebret, and did not explicitly determine whether in such a case the priest could, should or must be permitted to offer Mass. Apparently this point was left to the local ordinaries for further regulation wherever and

[163] *Dictionnaire de Droit Canonique,* III, 128.

[164] Vermeersch-Creusen, II, 42; *Dictionnaire de Droit Canonique,* III, 130; Regatillo, I, 63.

[165] Gasparri, I, n. 373; Van Hove, *Tractatus de Sanctissima Eucharistia* (2. ed., aucta et recognita, Mechliniae: H. Dessain, 1941), p. 337 (hereafter cited as Van Hove).

whenever circumstances necessitated such regulation.[167] Pre-Code jurisprudence was more concerned with the question whether a priest without a celebret could be permitted to celebrate Mass, than with the question whether he who had one was necessarily to be admitted to the celebration of Mass.[168] With regard to the latter question, however, at least one author immediately prior to the Code of Canon Law denied in general any such obligation on the part of the rector of a church.[169]

The legislation of the Code of Canon Law concerning the celebret is couched in positive terms—*Sacerdos . . . exhibens authenticas et adhuc validas litteras commendatitias . . . ad Missae celebrationem admittatur.*[170] How, precisely, is the term "*admittatur*" to be understood?

According to one commentator the celebret entitles the bearer to the privilege of offering Mass.[171] A number of commentators use expressions which at least imply that the bearer of a celebret has the *right* to be admitted to the celebration of Mass,[172] while other commentators explicitly mention and affirm this right.[173]

[166] Council of Chalcedon (451), canon 13—Mansi, VII, 377; c. 7, D. LXXI; Conc. Trident., sess. XXIII, *de ref.*, c. 16—Schroeder, *Canons and Decrees of the Council of Trent*, p. 445; S. C. de Prop. Fide, litt. encycl., 20 apr. 1873—*Fontes*, n. 4884.

[167] Gasparri, I, n. 373; Motry, p. 51.

[168] Simeone, "Il 'celebret' nel can. 804 e nella prassi," *Miscellanea Francescana*, XLIX (1949), 258, footnote n. 65; cf. Bouix, *Tractatus de Episcopo* (2 vols., Parisiis, 1859), II, 296.

[169] Many (1847-1922), *Praelectiones de Missa* (Parisiis, 1903), pp. 249-250 (hereafter cited as Many); cf. *Dictionnaire de Droit Canonique*, III, 127-128; cf. Simeone, "Il 'celebret' nel can. 804 e nella prassi," *Miscellanea Francescana*, XLIX (1949), 258.

[170] Can. 804, § 1.

[171] Ayrinhac, p. 85.

[172] Motry, pp. 51, 58; Blat, III, pars I, 108; Mothon, *Institutions Canoniques* (3 vols., Vol. II, Bruges, 1924), II, 73 (hereafter cited as Mothon); Romani, II, pars I, n. 195; Regatillo, I, 62; Cance, II, 256; Claeys Bouuaert-Simenon, II, n. 79.

[173] Pejška, p. 264; Raus (1881-1943), *Institutiones Canonicae* (2. ed., Lugduni: Vitte, 1931), p. 386 (hereafter cited as Raus); Ver-

The arguments given in substantiation of this latter interpretation, which one commentator regards as reflecting the common opinion,[174] are based on the use of the categorical word *"admittatur,"* which as a subjunctive clearly contains the idea of a command,[175] and the contrast between the terms used in the first and second paragraphs of canon 804, namely, *"admittatur"* and *"poterit admitti," "admitti potest."*[176] Thus it is manifest that the legislator intends to command recognition for the right to the admission to the celebration of Mass of the bearer of an authentic and still valid celebret. All things being equal, then, the rector of a church is obliged to permit a priest with a celebret to offer Mass in the church over which the rector has charge.[177] The exceptions to this rule will be considered in the next section of this dissertation.

In general, this obligation, positively considered, is binding until it meets with overruling circumstances of time, trouble and expense for the church's rector or for the church itself. Negatively considered, the obligation is such that aside from the circumstances just mentioned no local legislation can be effective against the admission legislated by the Code of Canon Law.[178]

meersch-Creusen, II, 42; *Dictionnaire de Droit Canonique*, III, 130; Coronata, I, 147; Cappello, I, 655; Simeone, "Il 'celebret' nel can. 804 e nella prassi," *Miscellanea Francescana*, XLIX (1949), 258; Eichmann-Mörsdorf, II, 44.

[174] Simeone, "Il 'celebret' nel can. 804 e nella prassi," *Miscellanea Francescana*, XLIX (1949), 258.

[175] *Dictionnaire de Droit Canonique*, III, 130; Simeone, "Il 'celebret' nel can. 804 e nella prassi," *Miscellanea Francescana*, XLIX (1949), 258.

[176] Coronata, I, 147.

[177] Blat, III, pars I, 108; *Dictionnaire de Droit Canonique*, III, 130; Simeone, "Il 'celebret' nel can. 804 e nella prassi," *Miscellanea Francescana*, XLIX (1949), 258.

For an interesting case concerning the obligation of a rector of a church to permit a priest with a celebret to offer Mass privately, even though the latter's refusal to offer a public Mass be unreasonable, cf. Mahoney, *Questions and Answers, The Sacraments* (London: Burns, Oates & Washbourne Ltd., 1946), p. 110.

[178] Motry, pp. 51-52; Cappello, I, 656; can. 804, §§ 1, 3. Cf. Chapter

The Code of Canon Law does not specify the number of times that the bearer of a celebret is to be admitted to the celebration of Mass.[179] Motry remarks that unless an authoritative interpretation is placed on the words of the canon that would limit the number of times or require the approval of the local ordinary after a certain number of times, there seems to be no reason why the rector of the church should limit the extent of the permission granted by the Code of Canon Law.[180] Most of the commentators consulted,[181] however, with the exception of one or two,[182] agree that the right of the bearer of a celebret to be admitted to the celebration of Mass and the corresponding obligation of the rector to admit him primarily concern the celebration of Mass during a transitory rather than a prolonged stay.

A disputed point is whether or not the rector is bound to supply to the priest with a celebret the utensils, that is, vestments, chalice, candles, and the matter necessary for the celebration of Mass.[183] In practice it is possible to distinguish and give norms for three possible situations. First, if there is no local custom regarding the matter and if ordinarily many traveling priests ask to offer Mass at the church, the rector is ordinarily not bound to supply gratis the utensils and matter necessary for offering Mass. This would be too great a burden. The local ordinary can exhort but not force the rector to do so.[184] Secondly, if there is no local cus-

V, Article 1, Section II, for a discussion of the character of the norms which the local ordinary may institute.

179 Can. 804, § 1.

180 Motry, p. 49.

181 Vermeersch-Creusen, II, 42; Van Hove, pp. 337-338; *Dictionnaire de Droit Canonique*, III, 130; Romani, II, pars I, n. 195; Claeys Bouuaert-Simenon, II, n. 79; Simeone, "Il 'celebret' nel can. 804 e nella prassi," *Miscellanea Francescana*, XLIX (1949), 258-259.

182 Eichmann-Mörsdorf, II, 44.

183 Cappello, I, 657; Regatillo, I, 62.

184 S. R. C., *Egitanien.*, 10 iun. 1602, ad III—*Decreta Authentica Congregationis Sacrorum Rituum* (5 vols. et 2 appendices, Romae: Ex Typographia Polyglotta, 1898-1927), n. 96 (hereafter cited as *D. A.*); S. R. C., *Soanen.*, 31 maii 1698—*D. A.*, n. 1999; S. R. C., *Nebien.*,

tom regarding the matter and if a traveling priest only occasionally presents himself for the purpose of offering Mass out of devotion or for some other reason, the rector is bound to supply the utensils and the matter for Mass, and the local ordinary can compel him to do so.[185] Otherwise the right given to a traveling priest by canon 804, § 1, would be of no practical value.[186] Also it would be unbecoming to refuse a request that is reasonable and conducive to the worship of God.[187] Thirdly, if there is the custom of supplying every traveling priest with the utensils and matter for celebrating Mass, this custom should be observed since it is reasonable and, in general practice, praiseworthy.[188]

A question which can fittingly be treated in this section concerns the conditions under which the rector of a church may demand a compensation or a fee for the utensils and matter furnished a visiting priest, with or without a celebret, for the celebration of Mass. Legislation on this matter is found in canon 1303, §§ 2, 3, 4. The conditions there must be simultaneously verified. It is postulated that the church be poor.[189] Some commentators hold that the church must be very poor.[190] But, since the rector of the church must have the permission of the ordinary to exact the fee, the question as to whether any individual church meets the condition envisioned by the canon would be decided by the ordinary.[191] Only those priests who celebrate Mass for their own conveni-

31 mart. 1703—*D. A.*, n. 2107; Gasparri, II, n. 672; Many, p. 250; *Dictionnaire de Droit Canonique*, III, 128; Cappello, I, 657; Regatillo, I, 62; Cance, II, 257.

185 Gasparri, II, n. 672; Many, p. 250; Cappello, I, 657; Regatillo, I, 62; Cance, II, 256-257.

186 Regatillo, I, 62.

187 Many, p. 250; Cappello, I, 657.

188 Cappello, I, 657; Regatillo, I, 62.

189 Can. 1303, § 2; Van Hove, p. 338; O'Brien, *The Exemption of Religious in Church Law* (Milwaukee, Wis.: Bruce, 1943), p. 35 (hereafter cited as O'Brien); Coronata, I, 147; Regatillo, I, 62; Cance, II, 257.

190 Ayrinhac, p. 86; Woywod, II, n. 1322.

191 Can. 1303, § 2.

ence in such a church are obliged to pay the fee.[192]

The fee is to be a moderate one and is to be determined by the bishop, not by the vicar capitular or administrator, nor by the vicar general without a special mandate. The bishop should fix the amount of the fee for the whole diocese, in a diocesan synod if possible, or, outside the synod with the advice of the chapter or the council of diocesan consultors, who must be heard for the validity of the act.[193] If only one or the other church requires the permission, the ordinary could determine the amount of the fee outside a synod and without the advice of the chapter.[194] A decree by the bishop establishing the amount of the fee must be observed by all, even exempt religious.[195] Anyone charging more than the decree allows would be guilty of a sin against justice and would be bound to restitution, at least in the case of a traveling priest with a celebret, since he has a right to be admitted to the celebration of Mass.[196] If no fee has been established by the bishop or by custom and a church belonging to regulars is poor, Vermeersch-Creusen hold that the religious ordinary could permit the exacting of a moderate fee in such a church, since the general term "ordinary" is used in canon 1303, § 2.[197]

Section II. "[*Sacerdos ... exhibens authenticas et adhuc validas litteras commendatitias ... ad Missae celebrationem admittatur,*] NISI INTERIM ALIQUID EUM COMMISISSE CONSTET, CUR A MISSAE CELEBRATIONE REPELLI DEBEAT."

A celebret can become invalid through any one of four causes, namely, through the completion of the period of time

192 Can. 1303, § 2; Ayrinhac remarks that the regulations of canon 1303 apply to the Masses of occasional visitors. For habitual celebration a special arrangement would be necessary.—Ayrinhac, p. 86.

193 Can. 1303, §§ 2, 3, 4; cf. can. 105.

194 Cappello, I, 658.

195 Can. 1303, § 3.

196 Cappello, I, 658; Motry, p. 58.

197 Vermeersch-Creusen, II, 438; Ferreres (1861-1936), *Compendium Theologiae Moralis* (13. ed., 2 vols., Barcinone: Subirana, 1925), II, 319; O'Brien, p. 35.

for which it was issued, through the non-verification of a condition upon which its validity depends, through revocation, or through the bearer's act of rendering himself unworthy to offer Mass. It is with the last of the four causes mentioned that this section of the dissertation is primarily concerned, although the revocation of the celebret will be briefly discussed at the end of this section. The clause, "*nisi interim aliquid eum commisisse constet, cur a Missae celebratione repelli debeat,*" of canon 804, § 1, determines the circumstances under which an authentic and otherwise still valid celebret becomes automatically invalid and inefficacious when the bearer has rendered himself unworthy to celebrate Mass.[198]

The term "*interim*" signifies that the priest has rendered himself unworthy to offer Mass *after* obtaining an authentic and valid celebret from the proper authority, and *before* the completion of the time-limit, provided that the celebret was issued for a definite period of time. Therefore, the time-limit as set in the celebret is of no further value once the bearer has rendered himself unworthy to celebrate Mass, the celebret is no longer to be considered valid,[199] and the bearer is not to be admitted to the celebration of Mass.[200]

The next point to be considered is how, according to canon 804, § 1, a priest renders himself unworthy to offer Mass. In general it is not a question here as to whether the priest is properly disposed for the celebration of Mass,[201] but rather it is a question as to whether he is externally worthy of that function.[202] The phrase "*eum commisisse*" implies some act —rather than an omission—which is often difficult to prove.[203]

Although the specific acts which would debar a priest from

[198] Cf. *supra*, pp. 39-42, for a discussion of the other causes which render a celebret invalid.

[199] Motry, p. 49; Duskie, p. 102.

[200] Augustine, IV, 131; *Dictionnaire de Droit Canonique*, III, 130.

[201] Van Hove, p. 337.

[202] Hannan, "Cases and Studies," *The Jurist*, VIII (1948), 453.

[203] Augustine, IV, 131; Blat, III, pars I, 108.

the celebration of Mass are not mentioned in canon 804, § 1, it is clear that the legislation there embodied includes not only delicts in the technical sense of the term,[204] but also any gravely sinful act, sufficiently known, of a scandalous or defamatory nature.[205]

If a priest incurs an excommunication,[206] a personal interdict,[207] or a suspension[208] which forbids the celebration of Mass, or if he incurs an irregularity resulting from a crime,[209] his celebret is *ipso facto* invalid. It can be mentioned here, even though the situations are not included in the ones envisioned by the part of canon 804 here being considered, that a priest who suffers from an irregularity rooted in some defect[210] or from a simple impediment to the exercise of orders[211] may not offer Mass.[212] In the event this occurs after he has obtained a celebret, the celebret becomes automatically invalid and inefficacious, even though there was no fault on the part of the priest.[213]

It is necessary to keep in mind also the meaning of the term *"constet"* with regard to the action by which a priest renders himself unworthy to offer Mass and causes the automatic invalidation of his celebret. It must be *morally certain* that the gravely sinful act was committed.[214] Any legitimate means of knowledge or proof could be utilized in the achiev-

[204] Can. 2195, § 1; Wernz-Vidal, IV, pars I, n. 72; Crnica, II, pars I, 37; Coronata, I, 147.

[205] Motry, p. 50; Cappello, I, 655.

Blat would include in these acts a serious sin that has not been confessed, even if the sin is occult, provided that the refusal to permit the guilty priest to offer Mass is occult.—Blat, III, pars I, 108.

[206] Can. 2261.

[207] Can. 2275.

[208] Cans. 2279, 2284.

[209] Cans. 985, 986.

[210] Can. 984.

[211] Can. 987.

[212] Can. 968.

[213] Can. 968.

[214] Blat, III, pars I, 108; *Dictionnaire de Droit Canonique*, III, 130; Cappello, I, 655.

Some commentators merely indicate that it must be *certain* that the act was committed, without specifying the type of certitude required.—Motry, p. 50; Ayrinhac, p. 85; Romani, II, pars I, n. 195; Cance, II, 256; Claeys Bouuaert-Simenon, II, n. 79.

ing of this moral certitude.[215] Knowledge obtained in confession is, of course, excluded.[216] Suspicions, unreliable statements or unsubstantiated reports concerning the conduct or attitude of a priest are not sufficient to keep him from offering Mass.[217] The legislator could have used a term which would have included the cases just mentioned. The fact that a rather restricted term is used does justice to the consideration that the number of unworthy priests is a relatively negligible quantity.[218]

When a priest, according to the norms just discussed, renders himself externally unworthy to celebrate Mass his celebret automatically becomes invalid and inefficacious in the sense that the rector of a church should refuse him admission to the celebration of Mass. The revocation of the celebret, however, would require an act by the competent superior.

The causes which result in the automatic invalidation of the celebret would be sufficient for the revocation of the celebret by the competent superior. Besides the acts or situations by which a priest, with or without fault on his own part, becomes unworthy to celebrate Mass, it is possible that other situations might arise in which the competent superior would desire to revoke the celebret of a priest. In all such cases the right of the priest to have a celebret and to offer Mass would have to be taken into consideration along with the other circumstances in the case.

Finally, once the cause for the automatic invalidation of the celebret is removed, it seems that the celebret would be valid once more, provided, of course, that the period of time for which it was issued has not yet been completed and any other conditions on which its validity depends are verified.

[215] Coronata, I, 147.

[216] Augustine, IV, 131; Coronata, I, 147; S. C. S. Off., decr., 18 nov. 1682—Denzinger-Bannwart-Umberg, *Enchiridion Symbolorum Definitionum et Declarationum de Rebus Fidei et Morum* (21-23 ed., St. Louis: Herder & Co., 1937), n. 1220.

[217] Motry, p. 50; *Dictionnaire de Droit Canonique*, III, 130.

[218] Motry, p. 50.

In case the celebret is revoked, the intervention of the competent superior would be required not only for the revocation of the celebret but also for the restoration of its validity or for the issuance of a new celebret.

CHAPTER IV

THE PRIEST WITHOUT A CELEBRET

Can. 804, § 2. *Si iis litteris careat, sed rectori ecclesiae de eius probitate apprime constet, poterit admitti; si vero rectori sit ignotus, admitti adhuc potest semel vel bis, dummodo, ecclesiastica veste indutus, nihil ex celebratione ab ecclesia in qua litat, quovis titulo, percipiat, et nomen, officium suamque dioecesim in peculiari libro signet.*

The Code of Canon Law has made the following provisions relative to the admission to the celebration of Mass by a priest without a celebret in a church other than the one to which he is attached:

1. If the rector of the church knows well that he is a priest in good standing, he may be permitted to offer Mass.

2. If he is unknown to the rector of the church, he may be permitted to offer Mass once or twice, provided he wears the ecclesiastical garb, does not receive any remuneration under any title from that church for the celebration of Mass, and enters his name, along with mention of his office and designation of his diocese in the book specially kept for that purpose.

Article 1. If the Priest is Known to the Rector of the Church.

Can. 804, § 2. *Si iis litteris careat, sed rectori ecclesiae de eius probitate apprime constet, poterit admitti; . . . .*

Canon 804, § 2, contains explicit legislation concerning the situation in which a priest without a celebret desires to offer Mass in a church other than the one to which he is attached. This legislation constitutes a favor[1] or an exception[2] with regard to the general principle, which is at least implied in canon 804, § 1, according to which a priest who

[1] Hannan, "Cases and Studies," *The Jurist,* VIII (1948), 454.

[2] *Dictionnaire de Droit Canonique,* III, 130; Blat, III, pars I, 108.

desires to celebrate Mass in a church other than the one to which he is attached should have a celebret.[3]

The supposition in canon 804, § 2, is that the priest asking to offer Mass has no celebret. Various reasons may exist in explanation of the lack of the celebret. The priest may not have secured one, or, in case he did, he may have forgotten or lost it,[4] or the one originally secured may no longer be valid because of the completion of the time-limit for which the celebret was issued.[5]

When the priest has no celebret, then, but the rector of the church knows well that he is a priest in good standing, he may be permitted to offer Mass.[6]

The term *"rectori ecclesiae"* is to be understood here in a broad sense, so that by the word "church" is meant every church and oratory wherein Mass can be celebrated,[7] and by the word "rector" is meant the priest who has charge of such a church or such an oratory, whatever his canonical status may be.[8]

Careful attention must be given to the phrase *"si . . . de eius* [*sacerdotis extranei*] *probitate apprime constet."* Some commentators are content with interpreting this to mean that the rector of the church must merely know the priest who has no celebret.[9] Likely, however, they mean to imply, as other commentators in so many words clearly state, that this knowledge must be of such a nature as to formally identify the priest as one in good moral standing in his own diocese,[10] and as a priest who is not excommunicated, suspended,

[3] *Dictionnaire de Droit Canonique,* III, 128; cf. Simeone, "Il 'celebret' nel can. 804 e nella prassi," *Miscellanea Francescana,* XLIX (1949), 262.

[4] Augustine, IV, 131.

[5] Cappello, I, 655; Romani, II, pars I, n. 196.

[6] Can. 804, § 2; Woywood, I, n. 699.

[7] *Supra,* p. 44. [8] *Supra,* pp. 45-46.

[9] Vermeersch-Creusen, II, 42; Claeys Bouuaert-Simenon, II, n. 79; Simeone, "Il 'celebret' nel can. 804 e nella prassi," *Miscellanea Francescana,* XLIX (1949), 264.

[10] Augustine, IV, 131; Mothon, II, 73; O'Brien, p. 166; Henry, p. 76; Woywod, I, n. 699.

personally interdicted, irregular or in any way impeded from offering Mass legitimately.[11] When such knowledge is had, the purpose of the law of the celebret is fulfilled.[12]

Concerning the priest who has no celebret, the rector of the church may have the required knowledge either through personal acquaintance or through the testimony of a competent third person.[13] This is in harmony with the pre-Code teaching on the matter under discussion.[14]

Likely a lesser degree of certitude would suffice in this case than in the one in which a priest with a celebret is to be refused permission to offer Mass because he has rendered himself unworthy to do so.[15] The former case is concerned with the granting of a favor, which point has already been indicated[16] and will be specifically treated later on in this article,[17] while the latter is concerned with the denial of a right which the celebret ordinarily gives to the bearer.[18]

[11] Raus, p. 386; Coronata, I, 147; Romani, II, pars, I, n. 196; Cappello, I, 655; Regatillo, I, 61; Cance, II, 257.

[12] Gasparri, I, n. 366; Blat, III, pars I, 108.

[13] Raus, p. 386; *Dictionnaire de Droit Canonique,* III, 130; Cappello, I, 655; Regatillo, I, 61.

With regard to the admission of a priest without a celebret to the celebration of Mass in a private oratory belonging to a lay person, it seems, contrary to Mothon's opinion, that the admission of such a priest should be under the control of another priest, even though the priest without a celebret is known to the one to whom the oratory belongs.—Mothon, II, 73. Cf. can. 804, § 2, which refers to the rector of the church as being the one capable of admitting a priest without a celebret to the celebration of Mass; cf. *supra,* pp. 46-47, where the question as to the one who is to examine the celebret of a priest who asks to offer Mass in a private oratory belonging to a lay person is discussed.

[14] Reiffenstuel (1642-1703), Lib. I, tit. 22, nn. 5, 6, 7; Leurenius (1646-1723), Lib. I, tit. 22, quaestio DCXLIX; Schmalzgrueber (1663-1735), Lib. I, tit. 22, n. 3; Giraldi (1692-1775), Lib. I, pars I, tit. XXII, sect. CXXXVI, cap. I; Devoti (1744-1820), II, 220, footnote n. 7; Santi (1830-1885), Lib. I, tit. 22, n. 3; Gasparri (1852-1934), I, n. 369.

[15] *Supra,* pp. 71-72. [16] *Supra,* p. 74. [17] *Infra,* p. 77.

[18] *Supra,* pp. 65-67; *Dictionnaire de Droit Canonique,* III, 130; Odia restringi et favores convenit ampliari.—Reg. 15, R. J., in VI°.

The phrase "*poterit admitti*" in the first part of canon 804, § 2, means that the rector of the church may permit the priest, if he has no celebret but is known to the rector as enjoying approved status, to offer Mass. This is a right which is given to the rector of the church by the Code of Canon Law.[19] By law, however, no strict right on the part of the priest to be admitted exists,[20] and hence there is no obligation on the part of the rector to admit him.[21] Nor, from the approach of legality, would the rector of the church be guilty of any injury or injustice in refusing permission in such a case.[22] On the other hand, no reflection is cast on a priest who is able to take advantage of the provisions of this part of canon 804, § 2, so that without having a celebret he may offer Mass in a church other than the one to which he is attached.[23]

Finally, whenever the rector of the church makes use of the provision of this section of canon 804, § 2, to allow the celebrating of Mass to a priest whose approved status is intimately known to him, there is no limit as to the number of times the rector may allow such a priest to celebrate Mass.[24]

Article 2. If the Priest is Unknown to the Rector of the Church

> Can. 804, § 2. *Si vero rectori sit ignotus, admitti adhuc potest semel vel bis, dummodo, ecclesiastica veste indutus, nihil ex celebratione ab ecclesia in qua litat, quovis titulo, percipiat, et nomen, officium suamque dioecesim in peculiari libro signet.*

If the priest without a celebret is unknown to the rector

[19] Simeone, "Il 'celebret' nel can. 804 e nella prassi," *Miscellanea Francescana*, XLIX (1949), 261-262.

[20] Raus, p. 386; *Dictionnaire de Droit Canonique*, III, 130; Coronata, I, 147; Regatillo, I, 61.

[21] Motry, p. 55; Ayrinhac, p. 85; *Dictionnaire de Droit Canonique*, III, 130; Cappello, I, 655; Cance, II, 257.

[22] Romani, II, pars I, n. 196.

[23] Blat, III, pars I, 108.

[24] *Dictionnaire de Droit Canonique*, III, 130; Regatillo, I, 61; Simeone, "Il 'celebret' nel can. 804 e nella prassi," *Miscellanea Francescana*, XLIX (1949), 264; cf. Coronata, I, 147; cf. Cappello, I, 655.

of the church, he may be permitted to offer Mass once or twice, provided he wears the ecclesiastical garb, does not receive any remuneration under any title from that church for the celebration of Mass, and enters his name along with mention of his office and designation of his diocese in a book specially kept for that purpose.

Section I. "SI VERO RECTORI SIT IGNOTUS, ADMITTI ADHUC POTEST SEMEL VEL BIS, . . ."

The second part of canon 804, § 2, provides for the situation in which a priest without a celebret is unknown to the rector of the church where he desires to offer Mass. All that is stated in the preceding article relative to the legislation of canon 804, § 2, being a favor or an exception to the general principle implied in canon 804, § 1,[25] relative to the supposition in canon 804, § 2, that the priest asking to offer Mass has no celebret and the possible explanations for this lack of the celebret,[26] and relative to the interpretation of the phrases *"rectori ecclesiae"*[27] and *"poterit admitti,"*[28] is applicable in this article of the dissertation.

The first point to be specifically treated in this article concerns the interpretation of the term *"ignotus."* Practically every commentator consulted merely repeats the term *"ignotus"* as used by the Code of Canon Law, or uses an expression which means the same thing, that is, that the priest in question is not known to the rector of the church.[29]

[25] *Supra,* pp. 74-76.

[26] *Supra,* p. 75.

[27] *Supra,* p. 75. The word *"ecclesiae"* is adverted to only implicitly in the second part of canon 804, § 2.

[28] *Supra,* p. 77. The phrase in the second part of canon 804, § 2, is *"admitti potest."*

[29] Augustine, IV, 131; Motry, p. 55; Blat, III, pars I, 108; Mothon, II, 73; Ayrinhac, p. 85; Raus, p. 386; Vermeersch-Creusen, II, 42; *Dictionnaire de Droit Canonique,* III, 130; O'Brien, p. 166; Romani, II, pars I, n. 196; Cappello, I, 656; Regatillo, I, 61; Henry, p. 76; Cance, II, 257; Claeys Bouuaert-Simenon, II, n. 79; Woywod, I, n. 699; Simeone, "Il 'celebret' nel can. 804 e nella prassi," *Miscellanea Francescana,* XLIX (1949), 264.

In reference to the word itself,[30] and the way in which it is understood by the commentators, then, it is evident that the situation here envisioned by the legislator is that of a priest who is not known to the rector of the church in any way, either through personal acquaintance, or through another person, or through other means.

It can normally be expected that not every priest without a celebret who desires to offer Mass in a church other than the one to which he is attached will be either entirely unknown to the rector of the church or known to the rector of the church in the manner described in the preceding article.[31] Likely there will be a certain number of priests concerning whom the rector of the church will have some knowledge, but not the knowledge that is postulated for permitting the priest to celebrate Mass indefinitely without a celebret.[32] In such circumstances at least the favor conceded by the legislator in that part of canon 804, § 2, which is here under discussion may be granted by the rector of the church.[33]

According to canon 804, § 2, the rector of the church may permit the unknown priest without a celebret to offer Mass "*semel vel bis,*" that is, once or twice. Only one commentator has been found who explicitly states that the phrase is not to be understood in its literal limitation.[34] At least two commentators restrict the permission to the celebration of two Masses.[35] The fact that most of the commentators,[36] however, simply repeat the words of the Code of Canon Law

[30] Can. 18.

[31] *Supra*, pp. 75-76.

[32] *Supra*, pp. 75-76.

[33] Cf. Romani, II, pars I, n. 196.

[34] Regatillo, I, 61.

[35] Raus, p. 386; *Dictionnaire de Droit Canonique*, III, 130; cf. Cappello, I, 656.

[36] Augustine, IV, 131; Motry, p. 55; Blat, III, pars I, 108; Mothon, II, 73; Ayrinhac, p. 85; Vermeersch-Creusen, II, 42; O'Brien, p. 166; Romani, II, pars I, n. 196; Henry, p. 76; Cance, II, 257; Claeys Bouuaert-Simenon, II, n. 79; Woywod, I, n. 699; Simeone, "Il 'celebret' nel can. 804 e nella prassi," *Miscellanea Francescana*, XLIX (1949), 264.

with no word of explanation leads one to believe that there is no reason to deviate from the usual signification of the phrase. Since the phrase usually means a little more than two and since the matter in hand is one of favor, to say that the rector of the church may permit an unknown priest without a celebret to offer Mass three times at the most does not seem to be going beyond the bounds of correct interpretation.[37]

Section II. ["... *Admitti adhuc potest*] ... DUMMODO, ECCLESIASTICA VESTE INDUTUS, ..."

The rector of the church may grant permission to an unknown priest without a celebret to offer Mass once or twice provided three conditions are verified.[38] The general purpose of these conditions is to render fraud improbable.[39]

The first condition is that the priest be wearing the ecclesiastical garb.[40] Since the request to offer Mass may often precede by as much as a day or even more the actual celebration of Mass, two distinct situations are possible. Commentators apply this condition to both. Thus, when the priest seeks the permission to celebrate Mass, he should be wearing the ecclesiastical garb,[41] which, as Motry indicates, is the minimum that can be required in the nature of an indication pointing to the clerical state. Even though this in itself is not a convincing proof, the absence of the garb in the case of an unknown priest is surely a cause for doubt,[42] except, perhaps, in some special circumstances. It is not required that the priest appear in the cassock,[43] or even in the ec-

[37] Can. 18; Regatillo, I, 61; Odia restringi et favores convenit ampliari.—Reg. 15, R. J., in VI°.

[38] Can. 804, §2; Motry, p. 55.

[39] *Dictionnaire de Droit Canonique*, III, 130.

[40] Can. 804, § 2. [41] Augustine, IV, 132. [42] Motry, p. 55.

[43] Blat, III, pars I, 108; cf. can. 136, § 1; cf. II Plenary Council of Baltimore (1866), n. 148—*Concilii Plenarii Baltimorensis II, Acta et Decreta* (Baltimore: Murphy, 1868); cf. III Plenary Council of Baltimore (1884), n. 77—*Acta et Decreta Concilii Plenarii Baltimorensis III* (Baltimore: Murphy, 1886).

clesiastical garb of the region where he is visiting, since clerical garb will differ in various parts of the world.[44]

Relative to the second situation, namely, the actual celebration of Mass, a decree of the Sacred Congregation of the Council, issued on July 28, 1931, indicates that the reference to the clerical garb in canon 804, § 2, primarily concerns the wearing of the cassock at Mass. Among other things, the decree prescribes that pastors and rectors of churches should not allow priests to celebrate Mass in their churches unless they are, according to canon 804, § 2, wearing the ecclesiastical garb, which garb is described in canon 811, § 1,[45] and consists of the cassock.

Section III. ["... *Admitti adhuc potest*...] DUMMODO ... NIHIL EX CELEBRATIONE AB ECCLESIA IN QUA LITAT, QUOVIS TITULO, PERCIPIAT, ..."

The second condition is that the unknown priest without a celebret receive nothing under any title whatsoever for the celebration of Mass from the church in which he offers Mass.[46] Conditioning the permission to celebrate Mass on the preclusion of any monetary gain to be derived therefrom by the priest without a celebret finds its basis in pre-Code legislation,[47] teaching,[48] and the condition specifically formulated by a pre-Code author,[49] and helps to preclude an unbecoming motive for the celebration of Mass.[50] This does not mean that the priest must celebrate a Mass for which he has no stipend either from some other person[51] or even

[44] Motry, p. 55; cf. Romani, II, pars I, n. 196.

[45] *AAS*, XXII (1931), 336-337; *Digest*, I, 123-125; Crnica, II, pars I, 37; Van Hove, p. 337; cf. Cappello, I, 656.

[46] Can. 804, § 2.

[47] Pope Innocent III (1198-1216)—c. 3, X, *de clericis peregrinis*, I, 22; Potthast, n. 2994; *supra*, pp. 12-13.

[48] Pirhing (1606-1679), Lib. I, tit. 22, n. 5; Schmalzgrueber (1663-1735), Lib. I, tit. 22, n. 3; Santi (1830-1885), Lib. I, tit. 22, n. 1.

[49] "... seclusa qualibet spe lucri, ..."—Santi, Lib. I, tit. 22, n. 1.

[50] Blat, III, pars I, 108.

[51] Raus, p. 386.

from the rector of the church. In case, however, the rector gives the priest a Mass stipend or an offering for celebrating one of the parish Masses, the money must come from the rector's personal funds.[52] As Raus (1881-1943)[53] pointed out in objecting to Mothon's seemingly strict view on the matter,[54] the Code of Canon Law does not forbid the priest to receive anything from any source whatsoever for the celebration of Mass, but only from the church in which he offers Mass. Thus as long as the priest receives no pecuniary remuneration whatsoever from the church itself, the condition under discussion is fulfilled.[55]

Section IV. ["... *Admitti adhuc potest* ...] DUMMODO ... NOMEN, OFFICIUM SUAMQUE DIOECESIM IN PECULIARI LIBRO SIGNET."

The third condition is that the unknown priest without a celebret write his name, mention his office and designate his diocese in a special book.[56] A priest religious could designate his religious house and its location. Canon 804, § 2, does not seem to require that this third condition be fulfilled prior to the celebration of Mass.

Several purposes are served by this condition. It provides an identification which, by means of modern communications or in some cases by the use of an official list of the clergy, could be quickly verified.[57] Further, it furnishes some kind of tangible evidence for later reference,[58] in case, for example, an ecclesiastical superior would find it necessary to take some action against the priest.[59] Finally, it would make it impossible, or at least more difficult, for an impostor to con-

[52] Motry, p. 55.

[53] Raus, p. 386.

[54] Mothon, II, 73.

[55] Motry, p. 55; Raus, p. 386; cf. *Dictionnaire de Droit Canonique*, III, 130.

[56] Can. 804, § 2; Motry, p. 55.

[57] Cf. *Dictionnaire de Droit Canonique*, III, 130.

[58] Motry, p. 55.

[59] Blat, III, pars I, 108.

tinue for a considerable length of time his work of fraud.[60]

No specifications as to the type or format of the special book are contained in the Code of Canon Law.[61] The book could be one which every visiting priest celebrating Mass in the church is asked to sign, or it could be a book set aside just for unknown priests without a celebret.[62] No mention of this book is made in the list of parochial record books in canon 470, § 1. Nor is the priest who has charge of the church obliged by the Code of Canon Law to send an authentic copy of this special book to the episcopal curia at the end of each year,[63] although he may be required to do so by reason of a diocesan statute or an episcopal regulation.[64]

[60] Motry, p. 55.
[61] Can. 804, § 2.
[62] Blat, III, pars I, 108.
[63] Can. 470, § 3.
[64] Motry, p. 56; cf. can. 804, § 3.

CHAPTER V

SPECIAL NORMS OF THE LOCAL ORDINARY

Can. 804, § 3. *Peculiares hac de re normae, salvis huius canonis praescriptis, ab Ordinario loci datae, servandae sunt ab omnibus, etiam religiosis exemptis, nisi agatur de admittendis ad celebrandum religiosis in ecclesia suae religionis.*

The Code of Canon Law has made provision for the establishment of special norms concerning the admission to the celebration of Mass of a priest in a church other than the one to which he is attached. These norms are 1) to be established by the local ordinary without prejudice to the prescriptions of canon 804; 2) to be observed by all, even exempt religious; 3) not to be considered as binding in the case of religious admitting members of their own institute to the celebration of Mass in a church of their own institute.

Article 1. Character of Norms Established by the Local Ordinary

Can. 804. § 3. PECULIARES HAC DE RE NORMAE, SALVIS HUIUS CANONIS PRAESCRIPTIS, AB ORDINARIO LOCI DATAE, [*servandae sunt . . .*].

The special norms established by the local ordinary concerning the admission of a priest to the celebration of Mass in a church other than the one to which he is attached must be observed. These norms must be established without prejudice to the prescriptions of canon 804.

Section I. "PECULIARES HAC DE RE NORMAE, . . . AB ORDINARIO LOCI DATAE, [*servandae sunt . . .*]."

The first two paragraphs of canon 804 contain the general law relative to the celebration of Mass by a priest in a church other than the one to which he is attached. The third paragraph of canon 804 refers to the enactment of particular laws or special norms in this regard.

These norms may be established only by the local ordinary,[1] and may be embodied in synodal statutes or, outside a synod, in episcopal ordinances.[2]

By nature these norms constitute more precise dispositions of the general law. Their purpose is to complement the general law and ensure its efficacy.[3]

This right of the local ordinary to establish norms regulating the admission of visiting priests to the celebration of Mass in his territory is a clear example of legislative power over travelers given to him by the Code of Canon Law.[4] Thus, in the case of extra-diocesan priests, canon 804, § 3, directly places non-subjects within the jurisdiction of the local ordinary.[5] A precise determination of those who are bound by these norms will be made in the second article of this chapter.

Section II. "[*Peculiares hac de re normae,*] SALVIS HUIUS CANONIS PRAESCRIPTIS, [*ab Ordinario loci datae, servandae sunt . . .*]."

The power of the local ordinary to regulate in his territory the celebration of Mass by a priest in a church other than the one to which he is attached is limited by the Code of Canon Law, which explicitly states with the phrase "*salvis huius canonis praescriptis*" that his norms must not conflict with the general law as enacted in canon 804.[6] This is an application of the principle that the local ordinary may make laws outside of *(praeter)* but not contrary to *(contra)* the general law of the Church.[7] Diocesan statutes, then, may supplement

[1] Can. 804, § 3; can. 198, § 2; Blat, III, pars I, 108.

[2] Mothon, II, 74.

[3] *Dictionnaire de Droit Canonique,* III, 131.

[4] Hammill, *The Obligations of the Traveler according to Canon 14,* The Catholic University of America Canon Law Studies, n. 160 (Washington, D. C.: The Catholic University of America Press, 1942), pp. 126-127 (hereafter cited as Hammill).

[5] Roelker, "The Traveler and the Local Statute," *The Jurist,* II (1942), 106, footnote n. 3.

[6] Can. 804, § 3; Motry, p. 56.

[7] *Dictionnaire de Droit Canonique,* III, 130.

the regulations of the Code of Canon Law relative to the matter under discussion, but may not contradict or annul them.[8] In other words, the prescriptions of canon 804, both positive and negative,[9] or with regard to what is commanded and what is permitted,[10] must remain intact and inviolable, and the general laws which determine the obligation of travelers with regard to special laws must be kept in mind.[11]

A consideration of the prescriptions of canon 804 will aid in specifying what norms the local ordinary may not and what norms he may enact.

First to be treated are the norms which the local ordinary *may not* establish. According to canon 804, § 1, a priest with an authentic and still valid celebret from the proper authority has a right to be admitted to the celebration of Mass,[12] unless it is morally certain that in the meantime he has rendered himself externally unworthy to offer Mass.[13] Therefore, prescinding from the exception mentioned, the local ordinary may not by a special norm prevent such a priest from celebrating Mass, for example, solely because he is from outside the local ordinary's territory.[14] Only in a particular case and for special reasons could the local ordinary prevent a priest with an authentic and still valid cele-

[8] Ayrinhac, p. 85.

[9] Cappello, I, 656.

[10] Blat, III, pars I, 108.

[11] Michiels, *Normae Generales Juris Canonici, Commentarius Libri I Codicis Juris Canonici* (2. ed., 2 vols., Tornaci: Desclée et Socii, 1949), I, 395; Van Hove, *Commentarium Lovaniense in Codicem Iuris Canonici*, 1 Vol. in 5 toms., Tom. II, *De Legibus Ecclesiasticis* (Mechliniae: H. Dessain, 1930), n. 220.

For a practical and interesting case in connection with the matter under discussion, cf. Canestri, "De lege cum sanctione poenali lata in peregrinos," *Consultationes Iuris Canonici*, II (1939), 14-20.

[12] *Supra*, pp. 65-67; cf. Cappelo, I, 656.

[13] *Supra*, pp. 69-72.

[14] Bouix, *Tractatus de Episcopo*, II, 296-297; Baart, *Legal Formulary* (3. ed., New York: Pustet, 1899), p. 153; Gasparri, I, n. 373; Wernz-Vidal, IV, pars I, n. 72, footnote n. 50; Motry, p. 56; cf. Vermeersch-Creusen, II, 42.

bret from offering Mass.[15] Nor may the local ordinary require that a priest present his authentic and still valid celebret to the local ordinary himself[16] or to the diocesan curia[17] for examination and approval before being admitted to the celebration of Mass in any church in his territory.[18] The Code of Canon Law makes no allusion to any such demand[19] and a requirement of this nature seems contrary to the spirit and letter of canon 804.[20]

Canon 804, § 1, does not place any limit on the period of time for which a celebret may be issued. The prescription of the local ordinary, then, that a celebret issued for more than a year or for an indefinite period of time is not to be accepted as still valid in his territory after six months or a year seems to be contrary to the general law.[21] Even if such a regulation were enacted, it would not interfere with the right of the rector of a church to admit a priest, whether known or unknown, with such a celebret or without a celebret, to the celebration of Mass according to the provisions of canon 804, § 2.

Since canon 804, § 1, indicates that a priest religious is to obtain the celebret from his superior,[22] the local ordinary

[15] Gasparri, I, n. 373; Wernz-Vidal, IV, pars I, n. 72, footnote n. 50.

[16] Simeone, "Il 'celebret' nel can. 804 e nella prassi," *Miscellanea Francescana*, XLIX (1949), 265.

[17] Pejška, p. 265; *Dictionnaire de Droit Canonique*, III, 129; Coronata, I, 147; O'Brien, p. 166; Cappello, I, 656.

[18] Such a requirement was permitted by the legislation previous to the Code of Canon Law.—Simeone, "Il 'celebret' nel can. 804 e nella prassi," *Miscellanea Francescana*, XLIX (1949), 265; cf. Ferraris, *Prompta Bibliotheca Canonica, Iuridica, Moralis, Theologica, nec non Ascetica, Polemica, Rubristica, Historica* (ed. novissima, 9 vols., Romae, 1885-1899), VII, 18.

For a discussion of the one who is to examine the celebret, cf. *supra*, pp. 44-47.

[19] *Dictionnaire de Droit Canonique*, III, 129.

[20] Simeone, "Il 'celebret' nel can. 804 e nella prassi," *Miscellanea Francescana*, XLIX (1949), 265.

[21] Simeone, "Il 'celebret' nel can. 804 e nella prassi," *Miscellanea Francescana*, XLIX (1949), 258; *supra*, pp. 39-41.

[22] *Supra*, pp. 50-56.

could not prescribe that such a priest present a celebret obtained from a bishop or another local ordinary.[23]

According to canon 804, § 2, the rector of a church has a right[24] to admit to the celebration of Mass a priest who does not have a celebret but who is known by the rector in the way envisioned by this part of canon 804.[25] The rector may not be deprived of this right by the legislation of the local ordinary in view of the provisions of canon 804, § 2, and the principle governing the norms established by the local ordinary—"*salvis huius canonis* [804] *praescriptis*."[26] The same must be said with regard to the right of the rector of a church[27] in the situation in which the priest without a celebret is not known to the rector of the church.[28] In this case, of course, the conditions imposed by the Code of Canon Law must be fulfilled.[29] The local ordinary, then, if he would prescribe that only a priest who has a celebret may be admitted by the rector of a church to the celebration of Mass, would be acting contrary to the provisions of canon 804.[30] Likewise, it is not within the power of the local ordinary to legislate that a priest without a celebret, whether known or unknown to the rector of a church, first get permission from the local ordinary or the vicar general or the episcopal curia,

[23] *Dictionnaire de Droit Canonique*, III, 131.

[24] *Supra*, p. 77; Motry, p. 56-57.

[25] *Supra*, pp. 75-76.

[26] Motry, pp. 56-57; Ayrinhac, p. 85; Ramos, "Celebración de sacerdotes forasteros," *Ilustración del Clero*, XXII (1928), 169-170; Coronata, I, 147; O'Brien, p. 166; Cappello, I, 656; Simeone, "Il 'celebret' nel can. 804 e nella prassi," *Miscellanea Francescana*, XLIX (1949), 264.

[27] *Supra*, p. 78.

[28] Can. 804, § 2; *supra*, pp. 78-80.

[29] Motry, pp. 56-57; Ayrinhac, p. 85; Simeone, "Il 'celebret' nel can. 804 e nella prassi," *Miscellanea Francescana*, XLIX (1949), 261-262.

It is evident that the local ordinary may not abolish by his legislation any of the conditions required by canon 804, § 2, for the admission to the celebration of Mass of an unknown priest without a celebret. Cf. Cappello, I, 656.

[30] *Dictionnaire de Droit Canonique*, III, 131; Coronata, I, 147; O'Brien, p. 166; Cappello, I, 656; Regatillo, I, 61-62.

since the Code of Canon Law gives the rector of a church the right to admit such a priest to the celebration of Mass.[31]

Another right which cannot be restricted by the legislation of the local ordinary is the right enjoyed by religious, according to canon 804, § 3, of admitting priests of their own institute to the celebration of Mass in their own churches without observing the special norms established by the local ordinary.[32]

It is fitting to make reference here to priests who come to a diocese to take up a collection. They must observe the norms of the Code of Canon Law[33] and of the II[34] and III[35] Plenary Councils of Baltimore with regard to the taking up of collections. That part of the law of the III Plenary Council of Baltimore, however, which forbade pastors to permit priests to offer Mass even once, when it is known that they have come into the parish for the purpose of taking up collections, seems contrary to the Code of Canon Law and therefore inoperative.[36] Canon 804 separates the qualifications for the celebration of Mass from those requisite for the taking up of collections. Furthermore, the rules which canon 804, § 3, authorizes local ordinaries to make seem to be those which assure the admission to the celebration of Mass of only those who are externally worthy of doing so. Therefore, to keep from offering Mass one who is known to have come into the parish to make a collection seems at variance with the provisions of canon 804, § 2, at least until an overt act of collecting has occurred.[37]

Finally it should be noted that very special circumstances

[31] Can. 804, § 2; *supra*, pp. 77, 78; Simeone, "Il 'celebret' nel. can. 804 e nella prassi," *Miscellanea Francescana*, XLIX (1949), 261-262.

[32] Simeone, "Il 'celebret' nel can. 804 e nella prassi," *Miscellanea Francescana*, XLIX (1949), 264.

[33] Can. 1503.

[34] N. 119.

[35] N. 295.

[36] N. 295; Hannan, "Cases and Studies," *The Jurist*, VIII (1948), 453; cf. *supra*, p. 62.

[37] Hannan, "Cases and Studies," *The Jurist*, VIII (1948), 453-454.

could induce the local ordinary to establish a special norm contrary to the provisions of canon 804. But, in every such case there is need of a special faculty from the Holy See for such derogation.[38]

The second point to be considered in this section has reference to the norms which the local ordinary *may* establish with regard to the matter treated in canon 804. Again it should be called to mind that such norms must be established without prejudice to the prescriptions of canon 804.[39] In their rôle of complementing the general law, these norms will better ensure its efficacy.[40]

The local ordinary may prescribe certain formalities through the observance of which there may be ascertained the authenticity of a celebret.[41] All priests, whether those with a celebret or those without a celebret but known to the rector of a church, could be required to sign a special register.[42]

A special norm of the local ordinary may order the rectors of churches to refer doubtful cases to the ordinary or to the episcopal curia,[43] without prejudice, however, to the obligations and rights of the rectors as delineated in canon 804.

Special regulations enjoining a visiting priest to notify the episcopal curia of his presence in the diocese,[44] or to pre-

[38] Cicognani, *Canon Law* (2. ed., Reprint, Westminster, Maryland: The Newman Press, 1949, p. 511 (hereafter cited as Cicognani); cf. Cappello, I, 656.

[39] Can. 804, § 3.

[40] *Dictionnaire de Droit Canonique,* III, 131.

[41] Ayrinhac, p. 85.

[42] Ayrinhac, p. 85; Raus, p. 386; *Dictionnaire de Droit Canonique,* III, 131; Regatillo, I, 62; Eichmann-Mörsdorf, II, 44.

[43] Drumm, p. 52. [44] Cicognani, p. 511.

A circular letter issued by the Sacred Congregation of the Council on July 1, 1926, concerns priests who for the sake of their health go on a vacation outside their own diocese. Such a priest must obtain permission for the vacation from his own ordinary, who is to inform the curia of the diocese in which the priest will be vacationing of the priest's coming, of the length of the vacation, and of the particular place where he will be staying. The priest, on arriving at his destination, is to present himself as soon as possible to the diocesan curia or

sent his celebret to the local ordinary or to the diocesan curia within or after a certain time are not at variance with the general law and must be faithfully observed.[45] Likewise, if the priest is going to be in the diocese for an extended period of time, he could be required to present his celebret to the curia every three or six months.[46]

One commentator holds that the local ordinary may limit the number of times that a priest without a celebret may offer Mass and that the local ordinary may rule that he be informed about the celebration of Mass by such a priest.[47] Likely the former opinion refers primarily to the celebration of Mass by a priest who is known to the rector of a church, since canon 804, § 2, states the number of times that a priest without a celebret and unknown to the rector may be permitted to offer Mass. When referring to the celebration of Mass by a priest without a celebret but who is known to the rector of a church, however, the Code of Canon Law places no limit on the number of times,[48] as the above mentioned commentator himself at least implies,[49] and other commentators definitely state.[50] The local ordinary, then, may only prescribe that he be informed of the celebration of Mass by a priest without a celebret but known to the rector of a church within or after a certain period of time.[51]

the dean or at least to the pastor, who is to report the matter to the local ordinary. The local ordinary or a delegate is to keep an attentive watch over the actions of the priest and not permit him to offer Mass unless all the prescriptions of the circular letter are observed.—*AAS*, XVIII (1926), 312; *Digest*, I, 138.

[45] Mothon, II, 74; Cicognani, p. 511; *Dictionnaire de Droit Canonique*, III, 131; Drumm, p. 52; Cappello, I, 656; Claeys Bouuaert- Simenon, II, n. 79; Eichmann Mörsdorf, II, 44; cf. Regatillo, I, 61; cf. N. 93—*Statuta Dioecesis Lacus Salsi Lata ac Promulgata in Synodo Dioecesana Prima, anno 1929* (Salt Lake, City, 1929).

[46] Bouix, *Tractatus de Episcopo*, II, 299; *Dictionnaire de Droit Canonique*, III, 131.

[47] Cappello, I, 656.

[48] Can. 804, § 2.

[49] Cappello, I, 655.

[50] *Supra*, p. 77.

[51] Cf. N. 30—*Code of the Diocese of Des Moines Decreed in the First Diocesan Synod, June 15, 1923* (Des Moines, 1923).

Finally, the local ordinary could with a special norm determine the priest from whom permission must be obtained by a visiting priest for the celebration of Mass in the oratories of pious houses.[52]

Thus it is seen that some special norms are evidently contrary to, while others are entirely in keeping with, the prescriptions of canon 804. It is clear that only the latter are obligatory in virtue of canon 804, § 3.

On the other hand, special norms may be established whose contrariety with regard to the general law as contained in canon 804 is not conclusively demonstrable. In all such cases, however, since the special norm has been established by competent ecclesiastical authority, the obligation to obey it is to be urged until an authentic interpretation would determine that such a norm has no binding character.

Article 2. Obligation to Observe Special Norms of the Local Ordinary

Can. 804, § 3. [*Peculiares hac de re normae,... ab Ordinario loci datae,*] SERVANDAE SUNT AB OMNIBUS, ETIAM RELIGIOSIS EXEMPTIS, ...

Concerning the obligation to observe the special norms established by the local ordinary according to the provisions of canon 804, § 3, relative to the law of the celebret, the general law formally asserts that these norms must be observed by all, including exempt religious.[53] In this matter, then, canon 804, § 3, with regard to extra-diocesan priests and exempt religious, directly places non-subjects within the jurisdiction of the local ordinary,[54] and constitutes an evident example of legislative power over travelers given to him by the universal law.[55]

By way of exception priests religious are not bound to observe the special norms of the local ordinary when a cer-

[52] Cf. N. 57—*Synodus Dioecesana Cincinnatensis Quarta, anno 1920* (Cincinnati, 1920).

[53] Can. 804, § 3; Augustine, IV, 132; *Dictionnaire de Droit Canonique*, III, 131; Claeys Bouuaert-Simenon, II, n. 79.

[54] *Supra*, p. 85.

[55] *Supra*, p. 85.

tain condition is verified.[56] This exception will be explained in the next article.

The main purpose of the present article is to indicate specifically those who are obliged to observe the norms established by the local ordinary and the circumstances under which they are obliged to observe them. These norms are binding, of course, only within the limits of the territory of the local ordinary.[57]

In general, they bind not only those priests who wish to offer Mass in a church other than the one to which they are attached, but also the rectors of the churches in which such priests desire to offer Mass.[58] In particular, these norms oblige all secular priests who wish to celebrate Mass in churches under the care of priests secular or religious, even exempt. Likewise, they oblige all priests religious, inclusive of such as enjoy a status of exemption, whenever they request permission to celebrate Mass in any church other than the one to which they are attached, be it under the care of priests secular or religious, even exempt, except in the case of priests religious who seek permission to offer Mass in churches of their own religious institute. Under the same circumstances and with allowance of the same exception, rectors of churches, whether secular or religious, even exempt, are bound to observe the special regulations of the local ordinary when they grant permission to celebrate Mass to any priests secular or religious, also when the latter enjoy a status of exemption.[59]

Article 3. Exception in Favor of Religious in a Church of Their Own Institute

Can. 804, § 3. [*Peculiares hac de re normae,... ab Ordinario loci datae, servandae sunt ab omnibus, etiam religiosis exemptis,*] NISI AGATUR DE ADMIT-

[56] "...nisi agatur de admittendis ad celebrandum religiosis in ecclesia suae religionis."—Can. 804, § 3.

[57] Blat, III, pars I, 108.

[58] Blat, III, pars I, 108.

[59] Augustine, IV, 132; Crnica, II, pars I, 37; Romani, II, pars I, n. 196.

TENDIS AD CELEBRANDUM RELIGIOSIS IN ECCLESIA SUAE RELIGIONIS.

In obliging all priests, even exempt religious, to obey the special norms established by the local ordinary relative to the law of the celebret,[60] the common norm provides for one exception.[61] This norm is not to be considered as binding in the case of religious when these admit members of their own institute to the celebration of Mass in a church of their own institute—"*nisi agatur de admittendis ad celebrandum religiosis in ecclesia suae religionis.*"[62]

When it is a question, then, of a competent priest religious, that is, of the priest who has charge of the church, admitting a visiting priest of the same religious institute to the celebration of Mass in a church of their own institute, neither the one admitting nor the one admitted will be bound to observe the special norms of the local ordinary.[63]

It is important to note that this exception applies to all religious, properly so-called, whether exempt or not,[64] and not merely to exempt religious, as some commentators at least imply.[65] The logical interpretation, that is, a consideration of the text and context,[66] as well as the grammatical structure favors the former opinion.[67] Thus the Code of Canon Law extends to all religious institutes a *privilege* which was formerly the prerogative of exempt religious only.[68]

In the term "priests religious," with regard to those who

[60] Can. 804, § 3; *supra*, pp. 92-93.

[61] Blat, III, pars I, 108-109; Mothon, II, 74.

[62] Can. 804, § 3.

[63] *Can.* 804, § 3; *supra*, pp. 92-93; *Dictionnaire de Droit Canonique*, III, 131.

[64] Cans. 804, § 3, 488, 1°, 2°; Augustine, IV, 132; Blat, III, pars I, 109; *Dictionnaire de Droit Canonique*, III, 131; Woywod, I, n. 699.

[65] Cf. Motry, p. 57, Ayrinhac, p. 85, and O'Brien, p. 166, who all seem to point to such a limited application.

[66] Cf. can. 18.

[67] *Dictionnaire de Droit Canonique*, III, 131.

[68] Can. 804, § 3; Augustine, IV, 132; Bouix, *Tractatus de Episcopo*, II, 292; Bouix, *Tractatus de Jure Regularium*, II, 188; S. C. C.,

may be admitted to the celebration of Mass according to the exception found in the common norm, there seems to be sufficient reason to include priests who are novices in a religious institute. Besides the arguments adduced previously in illustration of the claim that a priest who is a novice in any religious institute is to be included within the term "priests religious" in reference to the law of the celebret,[69] it can be mentioned here that the exception under discussion is in the nature of a privilege. Therefore, it seems permissible to include priests who are novices in a religious institute.[70]

Particular attention must be given to the interpretation of the phrase *"in ecclesia suae religionis"* as found in the statement of the exception under discussion.[71] For the interpretation of this specific point, as well as throughout this article, it is necessary to keep in mind that, although the matter is stated in the common norm by way of an exception,[72] yet it refers to a privilege, as was mentioned in the two preceding paragraphs.

When one deal with the phrase *"in ecclesia suae religionis"* (in a church of their own religious institute), and its use in the Code of Canon Law relative to the law of the celebret, it seems advisable to accept Schaefer's definition of a church of a religious institute (*"ecclesia religiosa"*). He includes in this term not only a church over which a religious institute has dominion or proprietorship, but also a church concerning which a religious institute has in a fixed and stabilized manner the care and direction.[73] This choice of an

Zacynthen., 27 iul. 1626—*Fontes*, n. 2471; S. C. de Prop. Fide, 28 iul. 1626—*Fontes*, n. 4433, footnote.

[69] *Supra*, pp. 52-53.

[70] *Dictionnaire de Droit Canonique*, III, 131.

At least one commentator requires that the priests be professed in a religious institute.—Blat, III, pars I, 109.

[71] Can. 804, § 3.

[72] Cf. can. 804, § 3.

[73] "Nomine ecclesiae Religiosorum (ecclesiae religiosae) non venit solummodo ecclesia, cuius dominium seu proprietas pertinet ad Religiosos, id est ad eorum Religionem, sed etiam eae, quae quadam sta-

acceptable definition excludes a detailed explanation of the dispute concerning what constitutes a title that gives a religious institute dominion over a parish church,[74] and at the same time it is in keeping with the object or end of the present law concerning the celebret.[75]

Thus the phrase *"ecclesia suae religionis"* with regard to the privilege mentioned in canon 804, § 3, includes not only churches and oratories, whether public or semi-public, when annexed to religious houses according to the norms of canon law and the respective constitutions of the religious institute, and oratories erected in houses or estates pertaining to religious even though they are villas, houses of vacation, etc.,[76] but also all oratories and parochial churches whose care and direction a religious institute here and now has according to some definite arrangement with the local ordinary.[77]

Finally, it should be remembered that when a priest religious seeks admission to the celebration of Mass in a church pertaining to secular priests or to religious of an institute other than his own, both he and the one admitting him are bound to observe the general law of the Church and the special norms of the local ordinary regarding the law of the celebret.[78] Likewise, even in the case of admitting a priest religious to the celebration of Mass in a church of his own

bili ratione subsunt moderationi et regimini alicuius religiosae familiae."— Schaefer, *De Religiosis ad Normam Codicis Iuris Canonici* (4. ed., Romae: Typis Polyglottis Vaticanis, 1947), n. 1220; cf. Vermeersch-Creusen, II, 328-329.

[74] *Petrinus,* "A Contract Determining the Status of a Religious Parish," *The Jurist,* IX (1949), 65-86; Gonzalez, *De Parocho Religioso Eiusque Superiore Locali,* The Catholic University of America Canon Law Studies, n. 313 (Washington, D. C.: The Catholic University of America Press, 1950), pp. 46-60.

[75] Can. 804.

For a general discussion of the meaning of *"ecclesia"* in canon 804, cf. *supra,* p. 44.

[76] Simeone, "Il 'celebret' nel can. 804 e nella prassi," *Miscellanea Francescana,* XLIX (1949), 264, footnote n. 73.

[77] *Dictionnaire de Droit Canonique,* III, 131.

[78] Augustine, IV, 132.

religious institute, the general law as found in canon 804, §§ 1, 2, with regard to a priest with or without a celebret, must be observed.[79] The privilege discussed in this article of the dissertation concerns only the non-observance, under the conditions described, of the special norms of the local ordinary relative to the law of the celebret.

[79] Augustine, IV, 132; Clancy, p. 133.

APPENDIX I

The following is a suggested form for the celebret. This form embodies all the elements pertaining to the celebret as discussed in Chapter III, Article I, Section I. It is fitting that the custom of writing the celebret in Latin be followed.

No..................

Omnibus has litteras visuris Salutem in Domino.

Harum tenore litterarum, fidem facimus atque testamur Rev. D. .... sacerdotem Dioecesis .... (monachum-sacerdotem Abbatiae ....), qui ex causa .... ad tempus .... a Nostra Dioecesi (Abbatia) aberit, esse bene moratum, integritate morum et vitae sacerdotalis probitate ornatum, nulla censura vel poena ecclesiastica aut irregularitate vel impedimento, quod sciamus, irretitum. Quapropter omnes locorum Ordinarios, in quorum dioecesibus commorabitur, ac ecclesiarum Rectores et Superiores in Domino rogamus, ut eundem Rev. D. ....ad Missae Sacrificium celebrandum admittant, humaniter recipiant, in cunctis tueantur.

In quorum fidem has litteras manu Nostra subscriptas sigilloque munitas dedimus.
Datae ex aedibus Nostris.

Die .... mensis..................

A. D. ....

(Loc. Sig.) ....

De mandato Reverendissimi Episcopi

....

Vicarius Generalis aut Cancellarius

APPENDIX II

The following is a copy of a document, testifying to a priest's good standing, which was issued by the Exarch of the Philadelphia diocese of the Byzantine-Slavonic Rite.[1]

Bishop's Chancery Office

SEAL

815 North Franklin Street
Philadelphia, Pa.
Date

No. ....

To Whom It May Concern:

This is to certify that the Rev. N.N. .... is hereby appointed by me, as Bishop of the Ruthenian (Ukrainian) Greek Catholic Diocese, pastor (assistant pastor) of .... Church in .... and as such he is duly authorized and empowered to celebrate the Holy Mass and administer the Sacraments to the Ruthenian (Ukrainian) Greek Catholic Faithful in the said cities.

✠ Constantine Bohachevsky,
Bishop.

[1] Henry, p. 77.

CONCLUSIONS

1. The form of the celebret is optional. (pp. 36-37)

2. A celebret which is so drawn up that it is recognized as such and which has the signature and the seal of the proper authority is to be considered authentic. (pp. 37-39)

3. The Code of Canon Law does not explicitly require that the celebret be issued for a specifically predetermined period of time. It is left to the prudent judgment of the authority issuing the celebret to determine the period of time for which the celebret is valid, if he places any time limit on it at all. (pp. 39-41)

4. The term "*sacredos extraneus*" does not refer merely to extra-diocesan priests. Of itself it also applies to any priest who is not legitimately connected in any way with the church in which he desires to celebrate Mass. (pp. 42-43)

5. The terms "*ecclesia*" and "*rector ecclesiae*" are to be understood in a broad sense in canon 804. (pp. 44; 45-46)

6. Canon 804 refers solely to the celebret of priests. (pp. 43-44)

7. The celebret is to be examined by the priest who has charge of the church where the visiting priest desires to offer Mass. (pp. 44-47)

8. It is possible to interpret the term "*sui ordinarii*" in canon 804, § 1, in such a way that it would include a local ordinary besides the ordinary of the diocese in which a secular priest is incardinated. (pp. 48-49)

9. A priest who is a member of a society without vows as described in canon 673 may obtain his celebret from his superior. (pp. 51-52)

10. A priest who is a novice in a religious institute or in a society without vows is to be included in the term "priest religious" with regard to the law of the celebret. (pp. 52-53; 94-95)

11. Unless the constitutions of a religious institute or of a society without vows provide otherwise, the local superior

is competent to issue the celebret for his subjects. (pp. 53-56)

12. A priest of an Oriental rite, when outside his own patriarchate or Oriental country he is subject to the jurisdiction of a local Latin or an Oriental ordinary of his own rite, may obtain a celebret from the respective ordinary in whose diocese he has established his domicile for the purpose of administering to the spiritual needs of the faithful of his own rite. (p. 60)

13. An authentic and still valid celebret issued by the proper authority gives the bearer the right to be admitted to the celebration of Mass. This right primarily concerns the celebration of Mass during a transitory stay in the place where the priest wishes to offer Mass. (pp. 64-69)

14. Canon 804 does not require that every traveling priest secure a celebret. Such a priest should have a celebret if he expects to be admitted everywhere to the celebration of Mass more than once or twice. Without a celebret he lacks all right to be admitted more than once or twice to the celebration of Mass. (pp. 64-69; 76-77)

15. A priest with an authentic and still valid celebret may be refused permission to offer Mass only when it is morally certain that since the celebret was issued he has by the commission of a gravely sinful act which would debar him from the celebration of Mass rendered himself externally unworthy to offer Mass. (pp. 69-73)

16. The rector of a church has the right, even in the absence of a celebret, to admit to the celebration of Mass any visiting priest whom he definitely knows to be in good moral standing in his own diocese and capable of offering Mass legitimately. Such a priest has no strict right to be admitted to the celebration of Mass. (pp. 74-77)

17. Likewise, the rector of a church has the right to permit a totally unknown priest without a celebret to offer Mass once or twice provided the conditions mentioned in canon 804, § 2, are fulfilled. (pp. 77-83)

18. The condition of canon 804, § 2, prescribing that a totally unknown priest without a celebret receive nothing under any title whatsoever for the celebration of Mass from the church in which he offers Mass does not forbid the priest to receive anything from any source whatsoever for the celebration of Mass, but only from the church itself in which he offers Mass. (pp. 81-82)

19. The local ordinary through the use of a special norm may not prevent a priest with an authentic and still valid celebret from offering Mass; nor may he require that a visiting priest present his authentic and still valid celebret to himself or to the diocesan curia for examination and approval before being admitted to the celebration of Mass in any church in his territory; nor may he deprive rectors of churches of their right to admit priests to the celebration of Mass according to the provisions of canon 804, § 2, be the priests known or unknown, with or without a celebret; nor may he restrict the right enjoyed by religious, according to canon 804, § 3, of admitting priests of their own institute to the celebration of Mass in churches of their own institute without observing the special norms established by the local ordinary. (pp. 86-89)

20. The local ordinary may invoke a special norm for prescribing certain formalities through the observance of which there may be ascertained the authenticity of a celebret; he may require all visiting priests, whether those with a celebret or those without a celebret but known to the rector of a church, to sign a special register; he may require visiting priests to notify the diocesan curia of their presence in the diocese or to present their celebret to the curia after a certain length of time; he may determine the priest from whom permission must be obtained by a visiting priest for the celebration of Mass in the oratories of pious houses. (pp. 90-92)

BIBLIOGRAPHY

SOURCES

Acta Apostolicae Sedis, Commentarium Officiale, Romae, 1909-1929; Civitate Vaticana, 1929—

Acta Ecclesiae Mediolanensis, a Sancto Carolo Cardinali S. Praxedis Archiep. Mediolan. Condita, Frederici Cardinalis Borromaei Archiepiscopi Mediolan. iussu undique diligentius collecta, et edita, 2 vols., Lugduni, 1682-1683. Tom. I, 1682; Tom. II, 1683.

Acta et Decreta Concilii Plenarii Baltimorensis III, A. D. MDCCCLXXXIV, Baltimore: John Murphy, 1886.

Acta et Decreta Sacrorum Conciliorum Recentiorum, Collectio Lacensis, 7 vols., Friburgi Brisgoviae, 1870-1892.

Bouscaren, T. Lincoln, *The Canon Law Digest,* 2 vols. and Supplement through 1948, Milwaukee, Wis.: The Bruce Publishing Co., 1934-1943-1949.

Bruns, Hermann, *Canones Apostolorum et Conciliorum Saeculorum IV-VII,* 2 vols., Berolini, 1839.

Bullarum Diplomatum et Privilegiorum Romanorum Pontificum Tauriensis Editio, 24 vols. et Appendix, Augustae Taurinorum, 1857-1872.

Code of the Diocese of Des Moines Decreed in the First Diocesan Synod, June 15, 1923, Des Moines, 1923.

Codex Iuris Canonici Pii X Pontificis Maximi iussu digestus, Benedicti Papae XV auctoritate promulgatus, Praefatione, Fontium Annotatione et Indice Analytico-Alphabetico ab Emo Petro Card. Gasparri Auctus, Romae, Typis Polyglottis Vaticanis, 1917; reimpressio, 1934.

Codicis Iuris Canonici Fontes, cura Emi Petri Card. Gasparri editi, 9 vols., Romae (postea Civitate Vaticana): Typis Polyglottis Vaticanis, 1923-1939. (Vols. VII-IX, ed. cura et studio Emi Iustiniani Card. Serédi).

Collectanea S. Congregationis de Propaganda Fide, 2 vols., Romae: Typographia Polyglotta S. C. de Propaganda Fide, 1907.

Concilii Plenarii Baltimorensis II, Acta et Decreta, Baltimore: John Murphy, 1868.

Concilium Plenarium Totius Americae Septentrionalis Foederatae, Baltimori Habitum A. D. MDCCCLII, Baltimore: John Murphy, 1853.

Corpus Iuris Canonici, ed. Lipsiensis secunda, post Aemilii Richteri curas . . . instruxit Aemilius Friedberg, 2 vols., Lipsiae, 1879-1881.

Corpus Iuris Civilis, 3 vols., Berolini, 1928-1929. *Codex Iustinianus,* quem recognovit et retractavit P. Krueger, ed. sterotypa 10., 1929;

Novellae, quas recognovit R. Schoell, et absolvit G. Kroll, ed. stereotypa 5., 1928.

Corpus Scriptorum Ecclesiasticorum Latinorum, 70 vols., Vindobonae, 1866—; Vol. XX, ed. A. Reifferscheid et G. Wissowa, 1890.

Decreta Authentica Congregationis Sacrorum Rituum, 5 vols. et 2 appendices, Romae: Ex Typographia Polyglotta, 1898-1927.

Decretales D. Gregorii Papae IX, suae integritati una cum glossis restitutae, cum privilegio Gregorii XIII, Pont. Max., et Aliorum Principum, Romae, 1582.

Decretum Gratiani emendatum et notationibus illustratum cum glossis, Gregorii XIII, Pont. Max., iussu editum, 2 vols., Romae, 1582.

Denzinger, Heinrich-Bannwart, Clemens et Umberg, Johannes, *Enchiridion Symbolorum Definitionum et Declarationum de Rebus Fidei et Morum*, 21.-23. ed., St. Louis: Herder & Co., 1937.

Duchesne, Louis, *Le Liber Pontificales*, 2 vols., Paris, 1886-1892.

Florilegium Patristicum, ed. Bernhardus Geyer et Johannes Zellinger: 44 fasciculi, Bonnae: Sumptibus Petri Hanstein, 1911-1941; Fasciculus VII, *Monumenta Eucharistica et Liturgica Vetustissima*, collegit, notis et prolegomenis instruxit Johannes Quasten, Bonnae, 1935.

Funk, Franciscus Xaverius, *Didascalia et Constitutiones Apostolorum*, 2 vols., Paderbornae, 1905.

———, *Patres Apostolici*, 2 vols., Tübingae, 1901.

Hardouin, Jean, *Acta Conciliorum et Epistolae Decretales ac Constitutiones Summorum Pontificum*, 12 vols., Parisiis, 1714-1715.

Hinschius, Paulus, *Decretales Pseudo-Isidorianae et Capitula Angilramni*, Lipsiae, 1863.

Jaffé, Philippus, *Regesta Pontificum Romanorum ab condita Ecclesia ad annum post Christum natum MCXCVIII*, ed. 2 correctam et auctam auspiciis Gulielmi Wattenbach curaverunt S. Loewenfeld, F. Kaltenbrunner, P. Ewald, 2 vols., Lipsiae, 1885-1888.

Liber Sextus Decretalium D. Bonifacii Papae VIII, suae integritati cum Clementinis et Extravagantibus, earumque Glossis restitutis, Romae, 1582.

Mansi, Joannes, *Sacrorum Conciliorum Nova et Amplissima Collectio*, 53 vols. in 60, Parisiis, 1901-1927.

Monumenta Germaniae Historica, Legum Sectio II, *Capitularia*, Tomus I, *Capitularia Regum Francorum*, denuo edidit Alfredus Boretius, Hannoverae, 1883.

———, Legum Sectio III, *Concilia*, Tomus I, *Concilia Aevi Merovingici*, recensuit Fridericus Maassen, Hannoverae, 1883.

Potthast, Augustus, *Regesta Pontificum Romanorum inde ab anno post Christum natum MCXCVIII ad annum MCCCIV*, 2 vols., Berolini, 1874-1875.

Schroeder, H. J., *Canons and Decrees of the Council of Trent*, St. Louis: B. Herder Book Co., 1941.

Statuta Dioecesis Lacus Salsi Lata ac Promulgata in Synodo Dioecesana Prima, anno 1929, Salt Lake City, 1929.

Sylloge praecipuorum documentorum recentium Summorum Pontificum et S. Congregationis de Propaganda Fide necnon aliarum SS. Congregationum Romanarum ad usum missionariorum, Romae: Typis Polyglottis Vaticanis, 1939.

Synodus Dioecesana Cincinnatensis Quarta, anno 1920, Cincinnati, 1920.

Thesaurus Resolutionum Sacrae Congregationis Concilii, 167 vols., Urbini, 1718-1741; Romae, 1741-1908.

REFERENCE WORKS

Achelis, Hans, *Die altesten Quellen des orientallischen Kirchenrechts. I. Die Canones Hippolyti*, Texte und Untersuchungen, VI, Leipzig, 1891.

Augustine, Charles, *A Commentary on the New Code of Canon Law*, 8 vols., Vol. IV, 2. ed., St. Louis: Herder, 1923.

Ayrinhac, H. A., *Legislation on the Sacraments in the New Code of Canon Law*, New York: Longmans, Green & Co., 1928.

Baart, Peter A., *Legal Formulary*, 3. ed., New York: Pustet, 1899.

Barrett, John D. M., *A Comparative Study of the Councils of Baltimore and the Code of Canon Law*, The Catholic University of America Canon Law Studies, n. 83, Washington, D. C.: The Catholic University of America, 1932.

Benedictus XIV (Prospero Lambertini), *De Synodo Dioecesana*, 2. ed., 4 vols., Mechliniae, 1842.

———, *Institutiones Ecclesiasticae*, Editio Tertia Latina Veneta, 2 vols., Venetiis, 1788.

Blat, Albertus, *Commentarium Textus Codicis Iuris Canonici*, 6 vols., Vol. III, pars I, Romae, 1924.

Bouix, D., *Tractatus de Episcopo*, 2 vols., Parisiis, 1859.

———, *Tractatus de Jure Regularium*, 3. ed., 2 vols., Parisiis, 1883.

Cance, Adrien, *Le Code de Droit Canonique*, 7. ed., 3 vols., Paris: J. Gabalda, 1946.

Cappello, Felix, *Tractatus Canonico-Moralis de Sacramentis*, 3 vols. in 6, Vol. I., 2. ed., Taurinorum Augustae: Marietti, 1928.

———, *Tractatus Canonico-Moralis de Sacramentis*, 5 vols., Vol. I, 5. ed., Romae: Marietti, 1945.

Cicognani, Amleto, *Canon Law*, 2. ed., Reprint, Westminster, Maryland: The Newman Press, 1949.

Claeys Bouuaert, F., et Simenon, G., *Manuale Juris Canonici*, 3 vols., Vol. II, 3. ed., Gandae et Leodii: Dessain, 1947.

Clancy, Patrick M. J., *The Local Religious Superior*, The Catholic University of America Canon Law Studies, n. 175, Washington, D. C.: The Catholic University of America Press, 1943.

Coronata, Matthaeus Conte a, *De Sacramentis Tractatus Canonicus*, 3 vols., Vol. I, Taurini-Romae: Marietti, 1943.

Creusen, Joseph-Ellis, Adam C.-Garesché, Edward F., *Religious Men and Women in the Code*, 4. ed., Milwaukee: Bruce, 1940.

Crnica, Antonius, *Commentarium Theoretico-Practicum Codicis Iuris Canonici*, 2 vols., Vol. II, pars I, Šibenik: Typis Typographiae "Kačić," 1941.

Devoti, Ioannes, *Iuris Canonici Universi Publici et Privati Libri Quinque*, 3 vols., Romae, 1803-1815.

Dictionnaire de Droit Canonique, Paris: Letouzey et Ané, 1924—.

Diederichs, Michael F., *The Jurisdiction of the Latin Ordinaries Over Their Oriental Subjects*, The Catholic University of America Canon Law Studies, n. 229, Washington, D. C.: The Catholic University of America Press, 1946.

Drumm, William M., *Hospital Chaplains*, The Catholic University of America Canon Law Studies, n. 178, Washington, D. C.: The Catholic University of America Press, 1943.

Duskie, John A., *The Canonical Status of the Orientals in the United States*, The Catholic University of America Canon Law Studies, n. 48, Washington, D. C.: The Catholic University of America, 1928.

Eichmann, Eduard-Mörsdorf, Klaus, *Lehrbuch des Kirchenrechts auf Grund des Codex Iuris Canonici*, 3 vols., Vol. II, *Sachenrecht*, Paderborn: Schöningh, 1950.

Feldhaus, Aloysius H., *Oratories*, The Catholic University of America Canon Law Studies, n. 42, Washington, D. C.: The Catholic University of America, 1927.

Ferraris, Lucius, *Prompta Bibliotheca Canonica, Iuridica, Moralis, Theologica, nec non Ascetica, Polemica, Rubristica, Historica*, ed. novissima, 9 vols., Romae, 1885-1899.

Ferreres, Ioannes, *Compendium Theologiae Moralis*, 13. ed., 2 vols., Barcinone: Subirana, 1925.

Fournier, Paulus-Le Bras, Gabriel, *Histoire des Collections Canoniques en Occident depuis les Fausses Décrétales jusqu'au Décret de Gratien*, 2 vols., Paris: Recueil Sirey, 1931-1932.

Gasparri, Petrus, *Tractatus Canonicus de Sanctissima Eucharistia*, 2 vols., Parisiis, 1897.

Giraldi, Ubaldus, *Expositio Iuris Pontificii iuxta Recentiorem Ecclesiae Disciplinam*, 2 vols., Romae, 1769.

Gonzalez, Franciscus J., *De Parocho Religioso Eiusque Superiore Locali*, The Catholic University of America Canon Law Studies, n.

313, Washington, D.C.: The Catholic University of America Press, 1950.

Gonzalez-Tellez, Emmanuel, *Commentaria Perpetua in Singulos Textus Quinque Librorum Decretalium Gregorii IX*, 5 vols., Lugduni, 1673.

Hammill, John L., *The Obligations of the Traveler according to Canon 14*, The Catholic University of America Canon Law Studies, n. 160, Washington, D. C.: The Catholic University of America Press, 1942.

Hefele, Charles-Leclercq, Henri, *Histoire des Conciles*, 11 vols. in 20, Paris: Letouzey et Ané, 1907-1949.

Henry, Joseph A., *The Mass and Holy Communion: Interritual Law*, The Catholic University of America Canon Law Studies, n. 235, Washington, D. C.: The Catholic University of America Press, 1946.

Hostiensis, Cardinalis (Henricus de Segusio), *Commentaria in Quinque Decretalium Libros*, 5 vols., Venetiis, 1581.

Ioannes Andreae, *In Quinque Decretalium Libros Novella Commentaria*, 5 vols., Venetiis, 1581.

Kurtscheid, Bertrandus, *Historia Iuris Canonici, Historia Institutorum*, Vol. I (ab Ecclesiae fundatione usque ad Gratianum), Romae: Officium Libri Catholici, 1941.

Leurenius, Petrus, *Ius Canonicum Universum*, 5 vols. in 4, Venetiis, 1729.

Loeb Classical Library, The, *Pliny Letters*, 2 vols., London: Heinemann, 1935.

Mahoney, E. J., *Questions and Answers, The Sacraments*, London. Burns Oates & Washbourne Ltd., 1946.

Many, Sebastianus, *Praelectiones de Missa*, Parisiis, 1903.

Michiels, Gommarus, *Normae Generales Juris Canonici, Commentarius Libri I Codicis Juris Canonici*, 2. ed., 2 vols., Tornaci: Desclée et Socii, 1949.

Migne, Jacques Paul, *Patrologiae Cursus Completus, Series Graeca*, 161 vols., Parisiis, 1857-1866.

———, *Patrologiae Cursus Completus, Series Latina*, 221 vols., Parisiis, 1844-1855.

Mothon, Joseph, *Institutions Canoniques*, 3 vols., Vol. II, Bruges, 1924.

Motry, Hubert Louis, *Diocesan Faculties According to the Code of Canon Law*, The Catholic University of America Canon Law Studies, n. 16, Washington, D. C.: The Catholic University of America, 1922.

O'Brien, Joseph D., *The Exemption of Religious in Church Law*, Milwaukee, Wis.: Bruce, 1943.

Panormitanus, Abbas (Nicholaus de Tudeschis), *Commentaria in Quinque Libros Decretalium*, 5 vols. in 7, Venetiis, 1588.

Pejška, Josephus, *Ius Canonicum Religiosorum*, 3. ed., Friburgi Brisgoviae: Herder, 1927.

Piatus Montensis, *Praelectiones Juris Regularis*, 3. ed., 2 vols., Tornaci, 1906.

Pirhing, Ernricus, *Ius Canonicum in Quinque Libros Decretalium*, 5 vols. in 4, Dilingae, 1722.

Raus, J. B., *Institutiones Canonicae*, 2. ed., Lugduni: Vitte, 1931.

Regatillo, Eduardus, *Ius Sacramentarium*, 2 vols., Santander: Sal Terrae, 1945-1946.

Reiffenstuel, Anacletus, *Ius Canonicum Universum*, 5 vols. in 7, Parisiis, 1864-1870.

Ristuccia, Bernard J., *Quasi-Religious Societies*, The Catholic University of America Canon Law Studies, n. 261, Washington, D. C.: The Catholic University of America Press, 1949.

Romani, S., *Institutiones Iuris Canonici*, 2 vols., Vol. II, pars I, Romae, 1944.

Rothoff, H., *Le Droit des Sociétés sans Voeux*, Brugis: Desclée de Brouwer, 1949.

Santi, Franciscus, *Praelectiones Iuris Canonici*, cura M. Leitner, 4. ed., 5 vols. in 2, Ratisbonae, 1903-1905.

Schaefer, Timotheus, *De Religiosis ad Normam Codicis Iuris Canonici*, 4. ed., Romae: Typis Polyglottis Vaticanis, 1947.

Schmalzgrueber, Franciscus, *Ius Ecclesiasticum Universum*, 5 vols. in 12, Romae, 1843-1845.

Schroeder, H. J., *Disciplinary Decrees of the General Councils*, St. Louis: B. Herder Book Co., 1937.

Stanton, W. A., *De Societatibus sive Virorum sive Mulierum in Communi Viventium sine Votis*, 2. ed., Halifaxiae: apud Custodiam Librariam Maioris Seminarii a Sanctissimo Corde B. V. M., 1936.

Van Espen, Zegerus Bernardus, *Ius Ecclesiasticum Universum*, 5 vols., Lovanii, 1753.

Van Hove, Alphonsus, *Commentarium Lovaniense in Codicem Iuris Canonici*, 1 vol. in 5 toms., Tom. I, *Prolegomena*, 2. ed., Mechliniae-Romae: H. Dessain, 1945; Tom. II, *De Legibus Ecclesiasticis*, Mechliniae: H. Dessain, 1930.

———, *Tractatus de Sanctissima Eucharistia*, 2. ed., aucta et recognita, Mechliniae: H. Dessain, 1941.

Vermeersch, A.-Creusen, J., *Epitome Iuris Canonici*, 3 vols., Vol. II, 6. ed., Mechliniae-Romae: H. Dessain, 1940.

Wernz, Franciscus Xaverius, *Ius Decretalium*, 6 vols., Romae 1898-1914.

Wernz, Franciscus-Vidal, Petrus, *Ius Canonicum ad Codicis Normam Exactum*, 7 vols. in 8, Vol. IV, *De Rebus*, pars I, Romae: Apud Aedes Universitatis Gregorianae, 1934.

Woywod, Stanislaus, *A Practical Commentary on the Code of Canon Law*, revised by Callistus Smith, revised and enlarged edition, 2 vols., New York: Jos. F. Wagner, Inc., 1948.

ARTICLES

Canestri, Albertus, "De lege cum sanctione poenali lata in peregrinos," *Consultationes Iuris Canonici*, II (1939), 14-20.

Hannan, Jerome D., "Cases and Studies," *The Jurist*, VIII (1948), 452-454.

Petrinus, "A Contract Determining the Status of a Religious Parish," *The Jurist*, IX (1949), 65-86.

Ramos, Domicio, "Celebración de sacerdotes forasteros," *Ilustración del Clero*, XXII (1928), 169-170.

Roelker, Edward, "The Traveler and the Local Statute," *The Jurist*, II (1942), 105-119.

Simeone, Lorenzo, "Il 'celebret' nel can. 804 e nella prassi," *Miscellanea Francescana*, XLIX (1949), 248-265.

Woywood, Stanislaus, "Answers to Questions," *The Homiletic and Pastoral Review*, XXXIV (1933-1934), 73-74.

PERIODICALS

Consultationes Iuris Canonici, Romae: Apud Custodiam Librariam Pontificii Instituti Utriusque Iuris, Vol. I, 1934; Vol. II, 1939.

Homiletic and Pastoral Review, The, New York, 1900—

Ilustración del Clero, Madrid, 1907—

Jurist, The, Washington, D. C., 1941—

Miscellanea Francescana, Rome, 1886—

ABBREVIATIONS

AAS—*Acta Apostolicae Sedis.*

Acta Ecclesiae Mediolan.—*Acta Ecclesiae Mediolanensis, a Sancto Carlo Cardinali S. Praxedis Archiep. Mediolan. Condita, Frederici Cardinalis Borromaei Archiepiscopi Mediolan. iussu undique diligentius collecta, et edita.*

Augustine—*A Commentary on the New Code of Canon Law.*

Ayrinhac—*Legislation on the Sacraments in the New Code of Canon Law.*

Blat—*Commentarium Textus Codicis Iuris Canonici.*

BRT—*Bullarum Diplomatum et Privilegiorum Romanorum Pontificum Tauriensis Editio.*

Bruns—*Canones Apostolorum et Conciliorum Saeculorum IV-VII.*

Cance—*Le Code de Droit Canonique.*

Cappello—*Tractatus Canonico-Moralis de Sacramentis.*

Cicognani—*Canon Law.*

Claeys Bouuaert-Simenon—*Manuale Juris Canonici.*

Clancy—*The Local Religious Superior.*

Coll.—*Collectanea S. Congregationis de Propaganda Fide.*

Coll. Lac.—*Acta et Decreta Sacrorum Conciliorum Recentiorum, Collectio Lacensis.*

Coronata—*De Sacramentis Tractatus Canonicus.*

Crnica—*Commentarium Theoretico-Practicum Codicis Iuris Canonici.*

CSEL—*Corpus Scriptorum Ecclesiasticorum Latinorum.*

Devoti—*Iuris Canonici Universi Publici et Privati Libri Quinque.*

Digest—*The Canon Law Digest.*

D. A.—*Decreta Authentica Congregationis Sacrorum Rituum.*

Drumm—*Hospital Chaplains.*

Duskie—*The Canonical Status of the Orientals in the United States.*

Eichmann-Mörsdorf—*Lehrbuch des Kirchenrechts auf Grund des Codex Iuris Canonici.*

Feldhaus—*Oratories.*

Fontes—*Codicis Iuris Canonici Fontes.*

Funk—*Didascalia et Constitutiones Apostolorum.*

Gasparri—*Tractatus Canonicus de Sanctissima Eucharistia.*

Giraldi—*Expositio Iuris Pontificii iuxta Recentiorem Ecclesiae Disciplinam.*

Gonzalez-Tellez—*Commentaria Perpetua in Singulos Textus Quinque Librorum Decretalium Gregorii IX.*

Hammill—*The Obligations of the Traveler according to Canon 14.*

Hardouin—*Acta Conciliorum et Epistolae Decretales ac Constitutiones Summorum Pontificum.*

Henry—*The Mass and Holy Communion: Interritual Law.*
Hinschius—*Decretales Pseudo-Isidorianae et Capitula Angilramni.*
Hostiensis—*Commentaria in Quinque Decretalium Libros.*
Ioannes Andreae—*In Quinque Decretalium Libros Novella Commentaria.*
Jaffé—*Regesta Pontificum Romanorum.*
JE—Jaffé, *Regesta Pontificum Romanorum,* ed. curavit Ewald.
JK—Jaffé, *Regesta Pontificum Romanorum,* ed. curavit Kaltenbrunner.
JL—Jaffé, *Regesta Pontificum Romanorum,* ed. curavit Loewenfeld.
Kurtscheid—*Historia Iuris Canonici, Historia Institutorum.*
Leurenius—*Ius Canonicum Universum.*
Many—*Praelectiones de Missa.*
Mansi—*Sacrorum Conciliorum Nova et Amplissima Collectio.*
MGH—Monumenta Germaniae Historica.
Monumenta—Monumenta Eucharistica et Liturgica Vetustissima.
MPG—Migne, *Patrologia Graeca.*
MPL—Migne, *Patrologia Latina.*
Mothon—*Institutions Canoniques.*
Motry—*Diocesan Faculties According to the Code of Canon Law.*
O'Brien—*The Exemption of Religious in Church Law.*
Panormitanus—*Commentaria in Quinque Libros Decretalium.*
Pejška—*Ius Canonicum Religiosorum.*
Pirhing—*Ius Canonicum in Quinque Libros Decretalium.*
Potthast—*Regesta Pontificum Romanorum inde ab anno post Christum natum MCXCVIII ad annum MCCCIV.*
Prolegomena—Commentarium Lovaniense in Codicem Iuris Canonici.
Raus—*Institutiones Canonicae.*
Regatillo—*Ius Sacramentarium.*
Reiffenstuel—*Ius Canonicum Universum.*
Ristuccia—*Quasi-Religious Societies.*
Romani—*Institutiones Iuris Canonici.*
Rothoff—*Le Droit des Sociétés sans Voeux.*
Santi—*Praelectiones Iuris Canonici.*
Schmalzgrueber—*Ius Ecclesiasticum Universum.*
Stanton—*De Societatibus sive Virorum sive Mulierum in Communi Viventium sine Votis.*
Van Espen—*Ius Ecclesiasticum Universum.*
Van Hove—*Tractatus de Sanctissima Eucharistia.*
Vermeersch-Creusen—*Epitome Iuris Canonici.*
Wernz—*Ius Decretalium.*
Wernz-Vidal—*Ius Canonicum ad Codicis Normam Exactum.*
Woywod—*A Practical Commentary on the Code of Canon Law.*

BIOGRAPHICAL NOTE

Geogre F. Schorr was born on January 6, 1920, in Lancaster, Ohio. He received his elementary and the first two years of his high school education at St. Mary's School in the same city. In 1936 he entered St. Charles Seminary, Columbus, Ohio. On the completion of his philosophical course there, he received the degree of Bachelor of Arts in June, 1942. In September of that year he entered Mount St. Mary of the West Seminary, Cincinnati, Ohio, for his theological studies. He was ordained to the priesthood at St. Joseph's Cathedral, Columbus, Ohio, on October 27, 1945. After two years of parochial work and teaching in Chillicothe, Ohio, he was assigned to chancery and parochial duties in Columbus, Ohio. Two years later, October, 1949, he was admitted to the School of Canon Law of the Catholic University of America. He received the degree of Baccalaureate in Canon Law in June, 1950, and the degree of Licentiate in Canon Law in June, 1951.

ALPHABETICAL INDEX

CANON LAW STUDIES*

327. Koesler, Rev. Leo J., O.S.B., J.C.L., Entrance into the Novitiate by Clerics in Major Orders (Canon 542, 2°).
328. McFarland, Rev. Norman E., J.C.L., Essential Conditions and Sufficient Signs of Vocation to the Religious Life.
329. Wiest, Rev. Donald Herman, O.F.M. Cap., S.T.B., J.C.L., The Precensorship of Books.
330. DeWitt, Rev. Max George, A.B., J.C.L., The Cessation of Delegated Power.
331. Mathis, Rev. Marcian John, O.F.M., J.C.L., The Constitution and Supreme Administration of Regional Seminaries Subject to the Sacred Congregation for the Propagation of the Faith in China.
332. Schorr, Rev. George F., A.B., J.C.L., The Law of the Celebret.
333. Sheehy, Rev. Robert Francis, A.B., J.C.L., The Sacred Congregation of the Sacraments: Its Competence in the Roman Curia.
334. Shields, Rev. Joseph A., A.B., J.C.L., Deprivation of the Clerical Garb.
335. Uricheck, Rev. George Edward, A.B., J.C.L., De forma celebrationis matrimonii in Ecclesiis Orientalibus ante Motu Proprio *Crebrae Allatae* et post.
336. DePauw, Rev. Gommar Albert Leo Julian Maria, J.C.L., The Legal Status of Catholic Elementary Schools in Belgium, 1830-1950.

* For a complete list of the available numbers of this series apply to the Catholic University of America Press, 620 Michigan Avenue, N. E., Washington 17, D. C.

www.ingramcontent.com/pod-product-compliance
Lightning Source LLC
LaVergne TN
LVHW050205080826
844660LV00012B/357

* 9 7 8 0 8 1 3 2 2 5 0 3 6 *